Mark Casto has touched on ministry need—hope for the  off! Drawing from deep st experience he lays out God's plan for those who have lost hope. Young and mature alike will be transformed by the message in this book. For those who preach and teach, there is help for reaching the present generation. I commend this book to all.

—Dr. Ron Phillips
Pastor, Abba's House
Chattanooga, Tennessee

I am deeply moved by the incredible revelation in *When Misfits Become Kings*. Mark Casto, a modern-day John the Baptist crying out to a generation, "Repent, for the kingdom of heaven is at hand," speaks to a generation that has been counted out. But just because man counts you out does not mean that God does. I know the feeling of being the baby in a family of twelve, feeling like the least among my people. Everyone said, "She will never amount to anything; she's shy, backward, and brown-faced." But God has a way of turning misfits into kings, or should I say "queens." You will be motivated by the pages of this book, as God has revealed so many revelations I wish I had had in my "misfit" days. Get ready for the royal robe, the crown, the ring, and most of all, the secret place where you have access to the King of kings. Get ready to reign!

—Judy Jacobs
Author, pastor, and worship leader

A divine decree has been placed on your life! God has called you to rule and reign with Him. However, many of you have felt rejected, dejected, and disjointed. You feel like a "misfit," but God has a way of reaching into the back side of the desert and finding a future king for His eternal purposes. This book will help you discover the path to kingship. As you read it you will access the keys that you desperately need to unlock your destiny. You don't have to remain a "misfit." This is your season to reign!

—Shane Warren
Pastor, The Assembly, West Monroe, Louisiana

Many of us fall short of the royal designs the King has planned for us, His kids. On life's journey, too often we're fed someone's head knowledge, which leaves us smarter—perhaps even more religious—but unchanged. Insights mined from the King's heart, however, carry His DNA and, when consumed, make us like Him. In *When Misfits Become Kings* Mark shows you how to take this journey for yourself and gives important tools and insights to help you along the way. This book is pregnant with God's majestic heart for you!

—Dutch Sheets
International prayer leader and conference speaker
Best-selling author of *Intercessory Prayer*

Mark Casto is an extraordinary gift that God has been grooming in the secret place of prayer for quite sometime. I had the privilege of fathering this young man daily for nearly four years. He travelled with me across this country and even other nations of the world. I saw in him, an Elisha, who is passionately pursuing the presence of God and the prophetic anointing to transform this generation. Since the moment I met him in West Virginia until this very day, Mark has stayed committed to the process of intimacy with the Lord, sharpening the gifts in his life, and keeping a heart of humility before God and man.

It is with great delight that I recommend this inspiring revelation *When Misfits Become Kings* to you as an anointed guide to help you navigate through the difficult places in life. You will receive dynamic insight into the secrets that God has given to faithful men and women who went from obscurity into influence. I thank God for such a manuscript, and I recommend that from the youngest to the oldest we hold these principles close to our hearts in order to see the synergy of generations come together in this last hour!

—Dr. T. L. Lowery
T. L. Lowery Global Foundation

WHEN
MISFITS
BECOME
KINGS

MARK CASTO

CHARISMA
HOUSE

Most CHARISMA HOUSE BOOK GROUP products are available at special quantity discounts for bulk purchase for sales promotions, premiums, fund-raising, and educational needs. For details, write Charisma House Book Group, 600 Rinehart Road, Lake Mary, Florida 32746, or telephone (407) 333-0600.

WHEN MISFITS BECOME KINGS by Mark Casto
Published by Charisma House
Charisma Media/Charisma House Book Group
600 Rinehart Road
Lake Mary, Florida 32746
www.charismahouse.com

To my wife Destani—you are the greatest example of Jesus I know. I'm grateful for your beauty inside and out! Thanks for believing that there is a king inside of a misfit like me.

CONTENTS

ACKNOWLEDGMENTS

There are a few wonderful people whom I would like to thank for walking with me through life. Many of the lessons shared came out of these vital relationships.

First, to Greg and Terri Casto, my father and mother who have loved me and supported me the whole way—thank you for raising me up to know the power and presence of God Almighty. Despite all that we have been through, we have learned to trust in Jesus. I know that you have always desired to give me more in the sense of this material world, but you gave me something this world could never offer. You showed me how to have a personal relationship with Jesus Christ. I love you.

I would also like to thank Barton Green for his time and talent. You are truly the most inspiring person I have ever met. Our times together will always be cherished. You literally caused my creativity to explode. I'm very thankful that you didn't allow me to go the easy route, but instead you challenged me to develop my ability as a writer and press through every barrier that blocked me. Without you this book would not have come together. Thanks for believing in me. The work you have done behind the scenes for countless men and women will be rewarded in eternity.

To Perry and Pam Stone, thank you for believing in me. What couple running an international ministry would decide to take in a ragtag group of young men and women and believe in them enough to buy property, build a building, and expand their ministry to reach the next generation, let alone to take me when I was only twenty-two years old and put me over the whole thing! You are like a mother and father to me. Thanks for seeing the potential in me and helping develop me into the person God wants me to be. I look forward to many more years of fruitful ministry together!

To Evan Kilpatrick, you have been a godsend in my life. I count you as a true friend, and I'm very thankful that you have answered the call of God to stand by my side in this season of my life. Not many men are willing to support and fight for another man's dream, but you have been faithful. You are a true, modern-day armor bearer with an incredible future in front of you. Your ability to shoulder the responsibilities in the ministry have freed me up to work hard on this book, and I thank you for that.

To Jessica Montgomery, the most incredible singer God ever created and thankfully a faithful assistant in all things. You are the only reason my life seems semi-organized. I want to thank you for believing in me and my entire family. Your friendship has been vital and is valued to this day for the way you have served us in the ministry and supported us in prayer. Thanks for loving us and serving this vision. I know I could not do all that God has placed in my heart without you. Destani and I love you more than you will ever know. You have helped this misfit "administrate" like a king!

To the Omega Center International family, I'm so thankful to be able to lead such a passionate group of people into the things of God. We are going to see every promise of God fulfilled and reach this generation by the power of God. It is an honor to serve you every week and see the work that God is doing in each one of you. I couldn't have asked for better people to run with in this incredible vision God has given us. Thanks for loving me and my family. Your words of encouragement and outpouring of support is the reason I keep moving forward!

And finally, to my wonderful wife, Destani Casto, thank you for being an amazing wife, mother, and friend. You are and will always be my dream girl. No one knows the sacrifice you make to support me, raise our babies, and help women believe that they are beautiful. You are a beautiful person inside and out. I found my good thing in you! This book and our ministry wouldn't be where it is today without your love and care. I love you.

FOREWORD

In 2009, following a major attack upon a close family member and nineteen overdoses in our small town of Cleveland, Tennessee, God began to deal with my heart concerning the next generation. While praying and asking the Lord for the future direction of the ministry, the Holy Spirit spoke and asked me, "Do you want to go where I am going?" Of course, the answer was, "Yes!" The Lord responded, "Then prepare to be a spiritual father to this generation, as I am going to pour out My Spirit on the sons and daughters." (See Joel 2:28–29.)

I thought to myself, "How will I father a generation? I am not a youth pastor. I am known as the prophecy preacher." Nevertheless, God led me to a small prayer and worship gathering led by a young man by the name of Mark Casto. I arrived there a few minutes before the service began and asked one of the greeters if I could speak to Mark. I was led to a small room where a group of leaders were praying, and I could sense the presence of the Holy Spirit. After they had finished praying together, I asked Mark to sit down, and the rest is history. We now co-labor together in what is now known as the Omega Center International.

Since the time we connected Mark and I have seen a small group of twenty-some young people turn into hundreds coming to our weekly gatherings, and thousands driving in from all over the country for our conferences. God has been gathering His people around His vision for this ministry with over eighty families from twenty-six different states moving to help us with the vision. This is just the beginning! We are starting to see the fulfillment of the Malachi 4:5–6 mandate, as my heart turned toward Mark and that small group of young people. Now we are seeing the bridging of generations, united around the move of God's Holy Spirit.

I have known Mark since he was only twenty-two years old. When I hear him preach, I and many of those who have known my ministry for years will comment that Mark reminds them so much of me in my twenties. It's no doubt that God connected me to this young man for such a time as this. He is a voice to this generation, with wisdom beyond His years, true revelatory preaching, and a powerful anointing to minister to all ages. I appointed Him as the pastor of the Omega Center International because he has an ear to hear what the Spirit is saying. He loves the church and is passionate about a generation having a tangible experience with Jesus Christ.

If you are not familiar with this young man or his ministry, get ready to be blessed. I know his life, his testimony, and his heart. This is not a message coming from a man who is just sharing an idea, but this has been walked out through personal experience and by revelation of the Holy Spirit. You will be challenged, encouraged, and inspired by this work. God has a special assignment for this generation. And no matter how misplaced or confused you are concerning God's purpose for your life, you are about to read truths that have the power to set your life in divine alignment for this last-day outpouring.

I love Mark Casto as a son in the Lord, and it is with great honor that I recommend not only his ministry to you but also his book, *When Misfits Become Kings*. The Lord has truly given Mark a message for this generation. So no matter what background you are from or how out of place you may feel, get ready—the Lord is looking for misfits that He can raise up to become kings.

Perry Stone leads Voice of Evangelism ministry in Cleveland, Tennessee, and hosts the weekly television show *Manna-Fest*. He is the best-selling author of several books, including *Breaking the Jewish Code* and *Purging Your House, Pruning Your Family Tree*.

INTRODUCTION

I was itching for adventure, but like many eighteen-year-olds I wasn't sure how to find it.

I knew that over the horizon, just beyond the city limits of my West Virginia town was a world of adventure just waiting to be explored. But looking in the mirror I saw a no-name kid from the sticks with few skills, no experience, and no foreseeable escape from my uneventful life.

In that hot summer of 2006, I was living with my folks, working a full-time day job, and going to night school. The drudge and repetition of it all made me feel like I was living a not-so-glamorous version of the movie *Groundhog Day*. Something in me longed for more, and I felt like a square peg in a round hole, an outsider, a misfit going nowhere very slowly.

Then someone called my name.

Turning toward the sound, I spotted a buddy from my church running toward me waving a flyer. Out of breath, he thrust the advertisement in my hand. "Mark!

This is it! You have to go with me!" The colorful brochure he was holding promoted a gathering called Dominion Camp Meeting, a four-day ministry event hosted by Columbus, Ohio, pastor Rod Parsley.

"C'mon, Mark, you need this," my friend urged. "You have to go with me—it will change your life!"

Given my mind-set, there was no need for a hard sell. He had me at the word *go*. But there was a hitch, actually a few of them.

I was broke. The air conditioning in my red minivan was busted, and I had no idea how I could afford the repairs, much less the trip. I didn't know where we would stay once we arrived or even if I would be able to take the needed time off from work and school. Yet despite all these obstacles in my way, the idea of attending the camp meeting tugged at my soul like a magnet. I couldn't explain it. Deep inside I felt like life—the life I longed for—was calling me.

I explained the situation to my parents, and after praying with them I approached my Circuit City manager for the four days I needed off. To my great surprise, he granted me the time requested with just a grunt and a nod.

Before I knew it, God had provided the time, the money, and even a place to stay in Columbus. Without any effort on my part, all the pieces of the puzzle came together. In those moments I felt I was the king of my domain. I was so excited it seemed I could run the five hundred miles to World Harvest Church on adrenaline alone. But thinking better of it, my friend and I laid our hands on the old minivan, said a prayer, and then hit the road for Columbus, Ohio.

That journey those many years ago not only transported me from my home state to Ohio, it literally transformed me from a West Virginia boy who felt out of place to a man who knew his purpose and life calling mentally and spiritually. That nearly thousand-mile round-trip journey took me places I had never been before, both on the map and within myself.

That memorable camp meeting shaped me. The sermons I heard preached there and the enlightenment I gained there showed this misfit that there was a plan and indeed a place where I perfectly fit. That Ohio gathering was where I first connected with my future and with the three men who over the years have separately and collectively guided me toward that "secret place" within that leads to great power and authority in God's kingdom.

The tale of that journey, those amazing men, and the lessons I have learned along the way comprise the content of this book. However, it is not my journey alone. It is one we all share.

At some point each of us has felt disconnected, unqualified, and alone, as if we are nothing but a square peg in a round world. Even so, our public surroundings do not have to define us. What we do in private, in secret, has the power to refine us. And that inward transformation has turned many misfits into the king or queen of their domain.

In these pages you will learn that your God-designed destiny is not controlled by your background or your social or economic status. Rather, it is unlocked through intimacy with the Creator of your future. In these pages you will gain a new perspective on where you fit in the jigsaw puzzle of life. You will learn how to discard your "misfit" pieces and fill that void with the power of intimacy we find in the secret place of the Most High. That is where opportunity begins.

In this book you will see how God can turn irrelevance into royalty and how rejection can lead to a coronation. You don't have to travel a thousand miles round-trip, as I did, to discover this. I believe your journey can be as simple as opening your eyes to the endless possibilities God has for you.

Don't be a square peg in this round world. Allow me to show you the secret to finding your path, your purpose, your place. When you do, that's when life really begins. That's when misfits become kings.

CHAPTER I

YOU ARE CHOSEN, IF YOU CHOOSE

Many are called, but few are chosen" (Matt. 22:14, MEV). Over the years this misunderstood verse has separated believers into two categories—the "chosen" and the "called." The chosen are the ones history remembers—the men and women whom God has used mightily and publicly. By contrast, those who are merely called tend to be the unnoticed, non-productive, second-rate citizens of the kingdom. Although such characterizations are far from the scripture's true meaning, the church has entertained this flawed comparison for generations.

Most folks use this verse to rationalize their role in the kingdom, or their lack of one. They tend to disbelieve that God has a purposeful plan designed just for them. They go about their daily lives unaware of their full potential and oblivious to their divine destiny. They simply shrug and shuffle through the day mumbling, "Some are chosen...I'm just called."

What a lie from the enemy! The actual Greek translation of Matthew 22:14 makes its meaning clear: "Many are called, but few choose to accept the call." The difference between being "called" or "chosen" depends simply on your willingness to choose.

Consider the case of John the Baptist.

This man's purpose was planned and prophesied before he was even conceived (Luke 1:13–19). In fact, on the very day he was circumcised, heaven spoke again of his future contributions (Luke 1:67–79). Indeed, every prophecy spoken or written about John was made before he was able to comprehend a single word. Still, none of these declarations would have come to fruition without John's willing collaboration. And that kind of spiritual cooperation comes only through a deep, intimate relationship with God.

In that secret place of the heart John and his Creator communed. In that personal, private place a spiritual relationship was forged, questions were formed and answered, and the first of many life-altering decisions was made.

Like John, when you spend time with God alone, "in secret," the public light of His blessings will never fail to illuminate your world. And your path will become a little brighter every day.

Just imagine what it was like for this uniquely spiritual man when the words of the prophet Isaiah first reached his ears in the synagogue: "The voice of one crying in the wilderness: 'Prepare the way of the LORD'" (Isa. 40:3). The hair on his arms must have stood on end when he realized that those ancient words, already centuries old, were calling out to him personally, unequivocally.

For any other man Isaiah's declaration would have been a dilemma, a real doozy of a decision: Who in his right mind would deliberately choose the wilderness as his "field of expertise"? No doubt the wheels of John's mind spun as he contemplated whether to obey or walk the other away.

Being the son of a well-respected priest, I'm sure John had more than a few prospects for gainful employment. But, ultimately, to be chosen was his choice.

Despite how illogical the option seemed, or how much of a misfit he appeared to the world, we know by the Scriptures that John chose to "make straight the way of the Lord" and follow the wilderness trail that God personally designed for him.

Making that choice to be chosen, John the Baptist literally became a man who was outstanding in his field. In doing so, this perceived misfit became the "king" of his domain. In fact, Christ Himself said as much when He described His forerunner this way: "Truly I say to you, among those who are born of women, there has risen no one greater than John the Baptist" (Matt. 11:11, MEV).

GREAT: PREPARED ON A GRAND SCALE

When Gabriel came to Zacharias and gave him the message that he would have a son named John, the angel said, "He will be great in the sight of the Lord" (Luke 1:15, MEV). The Greek word translated "great" is *megas*, which means "esteemed highly for his importance" and "prepared on a grand scale." And this is what God said about John before he was even born!

Likewise, before your birth, you too were prepared on a grand scale. You were already esteemed highly for your role in God's plan. Many have a hard time believing that we really matter to God, but just as it was with John, there is more to us than meets the natural eye. Something special has been placed within each of us. And it is more unique than our DNA.

Too few of us realize our "greatness" in God's kingdom, so we settle for being great in the sight of man. We strive for the glory of pleasing the world instead of pursuing the approval of the One who not only created this world, but personally knelt on the banks of its muddy shore and formed you after His own great image. You were not an accident. No one is a mistake. God had you in mind before the creation of time.

When the Creator called Jeremiah to be a prophet to the nation of Israel, He told him, "Before I formed you in the womb I knew you; and before you were born I sanctified you, and I ordained you a prophet to the nations" (Jer. 1:5, MEV).

It stands to reason that if God knew us before we had bodies, then our "greatness" does not come from our mortal frame, but rather from our eternal spiritual flame. Before you were formed inside your mother's womb, God took everything that you are—your gifts, abilities, passions, and desires—and made them permanent elements of your eternal spiritual character. Therefore, you can never become a product of your environment, for God Himself placed the source of your identity inside your spirit. So no matter how out of place you feel, you will never be a "misfit" for long.

The apostle Paul wrote, "For whom He foreknew, He also predestined" (Rom. 8:29). Knowing you intimately, and keeping in mind your purpose, God scanned all of eternity to find just the right time and place for you to shine. In His divine wisdom God placed you on this earthly chessboard in just the right position to take full advantage of your unique gifts. He chose for you to be right here, right now.

But keep in mind, overnight success never happens overnight.

God doesn't begin big works in public. He starts in secret, in that inner chamber of the heart, where the Creator teaches and molds an individual's "greatness."

John, for instance, was led to the obscurity of the desert to be prepared to change a nation. Of course, this goes against every success principle taught today. We are told to be strong networkers and to use all means of communication for promotion. But when God places His hand on someone, His initial plan is obscurity until that person's rare spirit is in tune with God's purpose. And when the timing is just right, the right individual will rise to right a nation.

Our present world is no picnic. Given the sad state of affairs today, it's apparent that we could use another John Wesley, another Charles Finney. But their time to shine has come and gone. Today's struggles are for us to combat. You were placed here and now with a purpose, for within you are the "great" solutions to the questions of this generation.

"Those whom He called, He also justified; and those whom He justified, He also glorified" (Rom. 8:30, MEV). However, at the moment you may feel overlooked, underappreciated, nothing but a square peg in a round hole—a misfit. If so, join the club. We all have been there. But when those feelings well up within you, remember the words of the psalmist, "It is God who judges: He brings one down, he exalts another" (Ps. 75:7, NIV).

And if anyone ever experienced that "rags to riches" roller coaster firsthand, it was the psalmist David.

THE FORGOTTEN BEGOTTEN

David's time to shine almost didn't happen. His rise from simple shepherd to Israel's second king was far from smooth. Of course, we all know the story. The tale of the young giant killer is the perfect example of God plucking a young man from obscurity and promoting him to lead. But as I reviewed the scriptural account of this now-famous king's early days, I happened across something I had never noticed before. And it was right at the beginning of the story.

Following the disobedience of King Saul (1 Sam. 15), God removed His favor from the throne and instructed Samuel to select a new king of Israel from the house of Jesse. On the appointed day, all the sons were invited to face Samuel for consideration—that is, all but one, Jesse's youngest.

This oversight has always bothered me. What compelled Jesse to leave David out of the process? Why would he deny his youngest the chance for a face-to-face encounter with Israel's greatest living prophet? Why would a father deliberately bar one of his sons from such a life-altering opportunity?

With my curiosity sufficiently stirred, I dug into both the Old Testament Scriptures and a selection of historic Jewish documents. In doing so I stumbled across a surprising backstory that is both subtle and profound. What I uncovered makes David's journey to the throne an even more amazing account than the "press release" version we've always been told. It is a story of Goliath proportions.

Jesse's decision not to include his youngest in the lineup had nothing to do with David being too young (Solomon was seventeen when he became king, and Josiah was only eight years old when he took the throne). Also, the boy's initial absence from the gathering had nothing to do with his assignment to watch the sheep. (The story of David and the giant begins with him bringing food to his brothers on the battlefield, so obviously there were *others* available to tend the flock.)

The real reason David was not invited to meet Samuel is shockingly simple: the shepherd boy was considered the black sheep of the family. He was the shunned one. The outcast. The misfit.

In the sixty-ninth chapter of Psalms, King David alludes to this family rejection with the words, "I have become a stranger to my brothers, and an alien to my mother's children" (v. 8).

A stranger? An alien? What terrible thing did David do to provoke his family to such disdain that it kept him from joining his brothers in that meeting with Samuel?

Simply put, David was born.

David wrote, "I was brought forth in iniquity, and in sin my mother conceived me" (Ps. 51:5). The "sin" David refers to here is not "original sin," which is the sin that we are all born into, but rather the specific sin that led to his conception, a deliberately deceptive act that had its beginnings two generations before his birth.

Paraphrasing the *Midrashim*, the body of ancient rabbinical exegesis of the Torah, David's little known backstory goes like this:

> David's father, Yishai, (Jesse) was the grandson of Boaz and Ruth (the couple's love story is detailed in the Old Testament Book of Ruth). Being aware of his family tree, Jesse not only knew the story but was haunted by the persistent rumors that had long questioned the legitimacy of his Moabite grandmother's marriage to Boaz.
>
> Being a student of the Torah, Jesse was aware that the sacred text forbade an Israelite to marry a Moabite (because that nation once refused the Jewish people passage through their land after their escape from Egypt). The law was strict and aggressively implemented against all Moabite males. However, when it came to a female Moabite, one who was willing to convert, the

rules were eventually relaxed, and the "mixed" marriages were quietly permitted.

When Jesse's grandfather, Boaz, declared his intent to wed Ruth publicly (Ruth 4:9), he did so hoping that his announcement would silence any objections to the amended law. However, he never got the chance to confront the unstoppable rumor mill that was about to begin, for the night after his wedding, Boaz died.

But apparently that one night was all that was necessary for Ruth to conceive. And in the fullness of time she gave birth to a son, Oved.

Even so, Boaz's sudden death sparked doubt in the minds of the suspicious, and before the mourning of the man ended, whispers about the woman began. *"Maybe the marriage to Ruth the Moabite should not have been allowed."* The murmurs and low chatter scattered the speculation, and over time the grapevine of gossip blossomed into an ongoing wives tale that had no apparent foundation, nor end.

By the time Oved's son, Jesse, had sons of his own, that whispered tale of illegitimacy was as much a part of the unwritten family lore as the Torah's listed "begats," which stretched clear back to Abraham himself.

Those whispered decades of doubt apparently gnawed at Jesse's integrity, wearing him down and sparking questions of his own about the purity of his ancestry. *"If this rumor is true and my grandparents' marriage was not legitimate,"* he rationalized, *"then I'm not legitimate—and my marriage to*

Nitzevet is certainly not lawful, for the Torah forbids a Moabite male from marrying an Israelite."

Entertaining this notion was a deception straight from hell. Nevertheless, this well-intentioned yet misguided train of thought led Jesse to no longer have marital relations with his spouse. Informing his children of his decision, he continued to provide for Nitzevet, but they lived separately.

After a number of years had passed, Jesse longed again for a child, one whose ancestry would not be questioned. So he made arrangements to wed his wife's Canaanite maidservant.

With the old rumor about his grandparents still on his mind, he informed his intended spouse, "I will free you conditionally. If my status as a Jew is legitimate, then you are freed as a proper Jewish convert to marry me. If, however, my line is blemished and I am but a Moabite convert, forbidden to marry an Israelite, you will remain a Canaanite maidservant, lawfully allowed to marry a converted Moabite."

The servant knew this news would upset her mistress. Over the many years of Nitzevet's banishment, the Canaanite had been a silent witness to the woman's painful separation from her husband and her prayerful longing for more children.

Empathetic to her mistress's situation, the maidservant secretly approached Nitzevet and not only informed her of Jesse's plan but boldly suggested a plan of her own. "Let us learn from your ancestors and replicate their actions," the Canaanite whispered. "Switch places with me tonight, just as Leah did with Rachel."

With a prayer on her lips, Nitzevet took the place of her maidservant. And that night, without Jesse being aware of the switch, Nitzevet conceived.

Three months later, Nitzevet's pregnancy became obvious. Incensed, her sons wished to kill their apparently adulterous mother and the "illegitimate" child she carried. But Jesse would not allow it. Upon learning of his wife's deceit, Jesse had compassion on her and ordered his sons, "Do not kill her! Instead, let us place the blame of the deception on her child. Let it be treated as a lowly and despised servant."

Therefore, from the day of David's birth his brothers treated him as an outcast. Noting the family's disdain, the townspeople likewise shunned him. If something was lost or stolen, David became the assumed culprit, and as in the words of the psalm, he was often forced to "repay what I have not stolen." (See Psalm 69:4.)

By everyone's estimation, the "legitimate" child that Jesse had longed for was now the least of his household. The son that he had hoped would become the salvation of his family's integrity was now nothing but a disappointment, an embarrassing misfit.[1]

In light of this amazing backstory it is obvious why David was not invited to his brothers' interview with Samuel. The boy was an afterthought, a castaway who spent more time in a pasture than with people. The very notion that someone of his perceived caliber could be a king was inconceivable—that is, to everyone but God, who made sure that David was conceived.

Being a misfit isn't necessarily a bad thing. Being shunned by the world can actually be a blessing in disguise. It provides one with the time and the elbow room to grow. Being banished to tend the sheep can be a great teacher of self-reliance, of how to think on your feet and lead others in a way that compels them to willingly follow. The solitude of a shepherd can offer one the freedom to practice an instrument, compose words and music, and learn the effective harmony of placing a smooth stone into a leather sling.

If David had been accepted as part of the family, he would have been pampered as a favored child instead of tempered by his battles with the animal predators in his pasture. Only by living as an outsider did he learn to depend on himself and the still, small voice of God within. Throughout his years among the sheep, that voice was his only genuine companion, his guide to greatness.

And it was that same voice that whispered to Samuel each time he lifted his horn of oil to anoint another of Jesse's sons king, *"No, not this one."*

By the time the prophet reached the seventh son, the room was tense, an emotional mix of anticipation, disappointment, and true bewilderment. No matter how high or how forcefully Samuel gripped his horn of oil, none of its contents escaped, not even a trickle. The prophet knew that he had been sent to Jesse's house to anoint the next king. Of this he was certain. But having vetted all the available candidates kneeling before him, none stood out of the crowd.

"The Lord has not chosen these," the prophet finally announced, turning to Jesse. "Are these all the sons you have?"

Jesse paused. Recalling his lifelong dream of an unquestioned ancestry, his hope of a legitimate son who would make everything right, and the deceptive switch that seemingly turned his plans to dust, the old man sighed. With a hint of embarrassment he pointed off toward the fields and mumbled, "There is the youngest. He is tending the sheep."

Samuel's face brightened. "Send for him. We will not sit down until he arrives."

When young David eventually walked into the large gathering, he was met by angry stares. But in the eyes of the only one whose opinion mattered, the boy was viewed differently. Recalling this pivotal moment, the Scriptures record that the boy was "glowing with health and had a fine appearance and handsome features. Then the LORD said, 'Rise and anoint him; this is the one'" (1 Sam. 16:12, NIV).

To everyone's surprise, the oil spilled out of the horn like a waterfall, cascading over the boy's head, through his hair, and onto his shoulders. And as the thick, rich liquid dried, I imagine it flickered gold in the candlelight forming a kind of crown on the shepherd's head. "And from that day on the Spirit of the LORD came powerfully upon David" (1 Sam. 16:13, NIV).

OBSCURITY IS AN OPPORTUNITY

Being a misfit isn't necessarily a bad thing. Being "discarded" can actually be the catalyst that reshapes the unwanted into the very one chosen to reshape the world. It can turn an outsider like John the Baptist into "the greatest among those born of women" and transform a family reject, put out to pasture, into a shepherd king chosen to lead the twelve united flocks of his own tribe.

If the wilderness John experienced is familiar to you, if you can relate to the years of rejection David endured, then you're not alone in feeling alone. Everyone who has ever accomplished anything has suffered through the growing pains of anonymity.

Your obscurity is your opportunity to develop your maturity—your greatness.

Both John and David used their "alone time," their separation from the world, to develop not only their uniquely personal gifts but to also strengthen their connections to the One who gave them both their design and their purpose. Each in his own way used his solitary days as a kind of "prayer closet." And though neither understood his future fully, what they did in their obscurity prepared them for their public roles.

Whether your alone time is in your private prayer closet or in the pasture you've been banished to, it is this personal private time with the Creator that will prepare you for your eventual premiere.

So make time for God. He literally created time for you.

At the moment no one may know your name or how amazing you are with your slingshot, but by no means are you the forgotten begotten. The Creator knew you before your birth. In fact, like David, God made sure you were born because your brand of greatness was tailored for the here and now.

Yes, there is a plan designed just for you. You are indeed called. But it's up to you to accept your assignment, to go through the obscurity that leads to maturity. For only you can choose to be chosen.

Today you have a reason to rejoice, for in the fullness of time, when your moment comes to shine, the oil will certainly flow. In the glow of God's guiding light His blessings will cascade over you like a waterfall of shimmering gold. And there will be no doubt that it forms a kind of crown on your head.

If you will simply choose to be chosen you won't be a misfit for long, because nothing fits like the crown made for you.

CHAPTER 2

WHERE ARE YOU?

W e all enter this world through nature's mortal portal. And the moment we arrive, we are each turned upside down, slapped on our backside, and rushed off to another room, away from our family. Is it any wonder we grow up confused about our place in the world?

But God knows. Before each of our births, He had our purpose and our path already mapped out. In fact, before the beginning of the world itself God not only had us in mind, He created a place where we could each individually walk, talk, and get acquainted with Him.

Strolling through Eden's garden alongside the Creator, Adam not only knew his place in the world but also his purpose. He belonged to God, and God belonged with him. Side by side, Father and son, Mentor and student, the two explored the plush paradise of Eden. Walking in the cool of the day, talking like friends, the duo were inseparable. Creator and creation truly enjoyed each other's company.

No one knows exactly how long that rare relationship existed. It could have been weeks, decades, or thousands of years. The only thing certain is that Adam chose to be chosen. He made time for God, for Adam knew that God literally created time for him.

Imagine it, the simple act of strolling with a friend, the only sound between them the in-sync rhythm of their feet swishing through the grass. Their slow, steady, casual pace was in perfect harmony with the surrounding beauty. The rhythmic subtlety of their steps was comforting, peaceful, and perfect.

Inside the boundaries of God's created Eden mankind had it made in the shade. Everything Adam and Eve could have ever wanted was within arms' reach. Walking on that path with God they knew nothing of prejudice, fear, or the pain of separation. In that paradise, all was right with the world. That is, until temptation slithered into the garden and lured God's chosen off their path.

The deceiver that caught the couple's attention that fateful day was Lucifer, the same fallen angel who was once an "anointed cherub." The apostle Paul referred to him as "the god of this world, [who blinds] the minds of those who don't believe" (2 Cor. 4:4, NLT).

This former angel once stood in the presence of God. In fact, to approach heaven's throne you would first have to pass by Lucifer, for his assignment was to "reveal" God, to point the way to the Almighty's divine presence. However, this once-regarded angel was swiftly removed from that position when his arrogance sparked a rebellion that pitted a third of heaven's angels against God Himself.

The cosmic battle that followed crushed the coup. And for his insolence, Lucifer was summarily booted from heaven and cast to earth.

From that vantage point, seeing God's obvious care for His newest creation, vindictive Lucifer set his sights on Eden's pair. Focusing his attention on their mortal weaknesses, the devil used his skills not to point the way to God (as he once did) but rather to misdirect humanity's attentions *away* from their Creator, in hopes that the same wrath God unleashed upon him would likewise be visited upon man.

I image that Lucifer, in the form of a serpent, slithered into the only garden tree that was off-limits, wrapped himself around a low-hanging branch, and did something to grab Eve's attention, like taking a bite out of the forbidden fruit himself. What better way to prove the fruit's power than for a "lowly creature" to take a nibble, then turn to God's highest earthly creation...and *speak*!

"Did God really say, 'You must not eat from any tree in the garden'?" The question's condescending tone planted the first seeds of doubt.

"No, just the tree in the middle," Eve replied, with a hesitant curiosity. "We can't even touch it, for if we do, we will die."

"You will *not* die," the serpent countered, taking another nibble. "God knows that when you eat from it your eyes will be opened, and you will be *like* God, knowing good and evil."

Ironically, in that conversation, the first found in the Old Testament (Gen. 3), the deceiver not only uttered the first of his many half-truths about God, but he also debuted the one seductive ploy he *still uses* today to toy with mankind: "*You will not die...you will be like God.*"

Without breaking a sweat Satan got the first couple to question their identity by dangling before them the one thing they desired most. It is his best trick, for the devil always manages to dangle the shiniest apple over the deepest pit.

His brand of misdirection not only lured a third of heaven's angels to rebel their way straight into hell, his practiced ploy was all Lucifer needed to detour Adam and Eve off the path God planned for them.

It was only two bites out of an obscure piece of fruit, but the act of reaching for the tree put paradise out of mankind's reach. It gave Lucifer a piece of forfeited ground to build on and turned the former "king and queen" of Eden into vagabonds, outcasts, the world's first... misfits.

An Unfamiliar Horizon

The half-eaten fruit filled his hand, yet in every way imaginable Adam was empty. I can imagine the scene. As the juice of his decision trickled off his chin, he felt disoriented and disconnected. The once familiar landscape surrounding him seemed strangely dark and foreboding. And as the full weight of what he had done settled over him, his knees buckled, threatening to drop Adam's naked frame back into the dust from which he was formed.

"Where are you?" The words came softly at first, like a whisper on the cool afternoon breeze. The inquiry seemed to come from every direction at once. Instantly Adam's eyes widened. Recognizing the voice, he felt the sudden thumping of his heart and he scanned the surrounding foliage for a place to hide. Frantically he tried to wipe the juice from his face.

"Where are you?"

The man didn't know which way to turn.

Just a few steps behind, Eve watched as her husband changed. His once-confident demeanor was gone. He appeared helpless, terrified—the same unfamiliar emotions that she too felt growing.

Both the whisper and the wind swelled, eventually howling through Eden's branches as if nature itself were angry. Chaos swirled everywhere. It surrounded them. It filled them.

Beneath the forbidden tree, Adam and Eve's choice had unleashed the knowledge of both good and evil into their veins. It opened their eyes to their own imperfections, their nakedness, and the undeniable superiority of God.

The whirl of it all compelled the two to run.

"Where are you?"

The Almighty's repeated question had nothing to do with the location of His creations. Their physical frames had no bearing on His inquiry. His concern was for humanity's soul, which was severed from Him the moment the man and woman sank their teeth into the forbidden. In that instant, God and His two companions were no longer in sync.

"Where are you?"

Adam and Eve didn't know which way to go, or how to answer the persistent question, because they no longer knew their own identity nor where the wind was pushing them. All they could do was run.

Eventually the weary two found themselves at Eden's end.

Having wandered out beyond the green grass, beyond the eastern gates of the garden, they stood facing an unfamiliar horizon of dirt, craggy rocks, and bushes made of thorns.

"Where are we?" Adam finally whispered, expecting no reply.

Feeling an unbearable emptiness, each took the other's hand and fought the urge to look back. Teetering there on the edge of oblivion, not knowing what to do, the two stood tearful but silent, not even turning when the windswept gates of their kingdom slammed shut behind them. "So He drove out the man; and He placed cherubim at the east of the garden of Eden, and a flaming sword which turned every way, to guard the way to the tree of life" (Gen. 3:24).

SQUARE PEGS IN A WHOLE NEW WORLD

Everything Adam and Eve had come to expect, every-thing they had taken for granted was gone in an instant. When they chose to eat from the tree of the knowledge of good and evil, they got just what they asked for. In a heart-wrenching moment, the two perceived the knowledge of every good thing they were now forced to leave behind, as well as the sudden consciousness of every evil that now surrounded them in their sudden, great unknown.

No longer were their days filled with leisure, playing in their backyard with Eden's menagerie of animals. No longer were their nights spent unaware of fear, the cold, and the dark. Having made their choice in the garden, they were now forced to make every decision for themselves.

Much like young David, who was exiled by his family to the outer pasture, Adam and Eve had no one to turn to but each other. The wilderness that replaced their once-beautiful surroundings was now their classroom, teaching them the cruel and often painful lessons of cause and effect. The supernatural garden they had so long taken for granted was now a rocky briar patch that was more raw "nature" than "supernatural."

Like every misfit who would come after them, the couple felt literally alienated—out of place. Life had changed. Their days of leisure were done. God told them, "By the sweat of your brow you will eat your food until you return to the ground, since from it you were taken; for dust you are and to dust you will return" (Gen. 3:19, NIV).

Hands that once reached for low-hanging grapes would become pricked and scarred by thorns. Feet that once walked on a carpet of grass would stumble over toe-stubbing shards of rock. Their days would become a repetitive 24/7 workout that would challenge muscles they didn't even know they had.

Thankfully, God still watched. Taking pity on their condition He slaughtered a lamb and clothed the couple before they were banished from the garden so they might have a protection against the elements and a measure of warmth against the cruel elements of the wilderness.

Each day outside Eden the man and woman would discover a new way to fall, and a better way to get back up again. Over time, such constant reoccurring mistakes reminded them of the often-painful consequences of their actions. And eventually these painful moments were repeated enough that they devised a better way.

Through this daily drudge of trial and error Adam and Eve not only discovered how to approach their tasks more efficiently, but they learned that their attempted shortcuts did not always produce the desired results. In other words, the short, easy way did not improve their hostile surroundings as well as the muscle-aching, character-building efforts of genuine hard work.

Such cruel but necessary reconditioning left them weary, but wiser.

Slowly, painfully, they learned the rules of their new surroundings. And eventually they passed along their hard-earned knowledge to the next generation.

To their firstborn, Cain, the couple taught the art of sowing and reaping, how to plow, plant, weed, and harvest. Growing up on this obstacle course, Cain spent his early days listening to his father coach him in the art of farming. Day after day he endured the training of Adam's verbal instructions in the field and the many diagrams drawn in the dirt. The life of Earth's firstborn was a perpetual cycle of backbreaking labor. Day after week after year, Cain plowed, planted, and weeded in man's attempt to replicate the garden.

His brother, Abel, was likewise trained by his parents. And like every generation that would come afterward, the younger took the instructions of his elders and spun that knowledge off his own way. Applying that filed-away knowledge to his life, Abel chose the vocation of shepherd, the keeper of the flocks that provided the wool to cover their bodies and the blood to cover their transgressions. Herding, feeding, and protecting a vast flock of sheep was a far cry from the easygoing days of Eden. It demanded of Abel just as much diligence, dedication, and perspiration as Cain's field of vegetables.

"Abel kept flocks, and Cain worked the soil" (Gen. 4:2, NIV). I imagine that after a long day, the family would gather around the evening campfire. There, the brothers would listen as their parents told again and again the story of God and the garden. I don't believe the couple would have held anything back. They summoned the memory of their past because they wanted their boys to evaluate what they had done and choose a better way for their lives.

Reenacting the moment when the serpent said, "*You will be like God,*" Eve would stretch her arm up, as if reaching for the tree. Even in the flickering firelight the message was clear: they chose what was easy (their selfish desire) over what they thought was hard (resisting temptation), and discovered that the easy way wasn't the easy way.

It was a painful lesson, a cruel but necessary effort on the behalf of the couple to be kind to their offspring, for it is the hope of every parent that their example will help to make their children wiser. Yet as Adam and Eve sought to somehow keep their children from feeling out of place, their heavenly Father was working on a plan for them. Little did they know that the lamb's skin they were wearing was the prophetic sign of man's process to reign as kings and be in divine relationship with God once again.

CHAPTER 3

PASSWORD: PASSOVER LAMB

Due to the sensitivity of information now available electronically, almost everything is password protected, from our cell phones and tablet computers to our e-mail and bank accounts. A password proves authentication of identity or approval to gain access to a resource, and we know it should be kept secret from those who are not allowed access.

What exactly does this have to do with God's plan to bring mankind back into divine relationship? Simply this: because Adam and Eve were banished from the garden, we must now gain approval or authentication of identity to regain access to God's presence.

Adam's sense of identity and his assurance of the reason for his existence came from walking and talking with the Creator in the garden. But now he and Eve were banished from Eden, they were lost and out of step with God. Yet the Creator longed for us to again have intimate fellowship with Him. So He decided to create a password that would allow us to regain access to the tree of life.

If you bank online, you are aware that when setting up the password for your account, you must provide a hint. That's because there will be times when you won't remember the password exactly. In Genesis 3:21, the Creator leaves us with a hint for the password He set up. As we read in the previous chapter, before God banished Adam and Eve, He clothed them in animal skins. Those were not the skins of just any animal. Many reference sources, theologians, and even rabbinical literature suggest that God slew a lamb in the garden and clothed Adam and Eve with its skin.

What is the significance of the lamb? It is the hint to the password that will allow us to access Eden, the place of intimate fellowship with the Creator.

The slaughter of this innocent creature instituted the practice of animal sacrifice. It was God's way of showing Adam that there was a price for his disobedience. The cost of man's sinful act was the forfeiture of creation's most valuable commodity, the very essence of life itself—blood.

Imagine the first sacrifice. From among his fellow residents in the garden, Adam had to choose one animal to die—not because of anything it did, but rather because of the one act Adam committed. The sanctioned practice of deliberately spilling creation's most valuable commodity was God's ultimate hint to the password that would return full access to His presence.

But this Old Testament form of sacrifice had to be reenacted frequently, for animal blood was never full restitution for mankind's crime. To pay the price for sin once and for all, God planned something special. On a very special sacrificial day the valuable essence spilled would stain a wooden cross and become the key that unlocks Eden's gate, allowing man unfettered access to God once more.

The blood of that final sacrifice would come from a man who would choose to be chosen—a banished man, an outcast from the establishment, a man shunned by His own tribe. The valuable essence shed on that day would cascade like a waterfall through the outcast's hair. And like the oil that flowed on David's head the day he was anointed king, this flood would form a kind of crown, anointing this chosen one. A man considered a misfit would become the King of every tribe.

In Genesis 4:26 the Bible says "men began to call on the name of the LORD" (MEV). This shows a transition taking place after Adam and Eve were banished from Eden. As long as there was blood on the altar man could access the presence of God again.

As the generations passed, a remnant of men continued to walk with God, experiencing the life-sustaining power of intimacy with the Creator. This remnant found favor in the eyes of the Lord because of their obedience to His will revealed to them personally and because they faithfully sacrificed animals to atone for their sins.

These men and women called on the name of the Lord because they recognized their need to be obedient and sacrifice the blood of animals to atone for their sins. The sacrifice of animals as a means of being made right before God produced a deep longing for Eden in the hearts of mankind. Nevertheless, sin kept drawing people's hearts to the things of this world and eventually led to God's chosen people, Israel, living in bondage in Egypt.

Moses, a Hebrew child whom Pharaoh's daughter rescued, was raised in the very house of Pharaoh but became a convicted murderer in Egypt. Like Adam, he too was a banished misfit, escaping to the back side of the desert, to Horeb, the mountain of God, where he tended his father-in-law's sheep.

While assuming the usual responsibilities of sheep-herding, Moses noticed a bush that was burning and yet not consumed. I think this is something to ponder, because we know that in Adam's banishment an angel stood guard with a sword of fire to keep people from the way to the tree of life (Gen. 3:22–24). And now in Exodus 3, the angel of the Lord appears to Moses in a flame of fire from the midst of something that grows in gardens—a bush.

Could this have been an invitation from Eden, the place where God gave mankind his identity and purpose?

The Creator's first words were, "Moses, Moses!" In that moment God not only knew Moses's name but also his purpose: for him to return to Egypt to deliver His people. God spoke to Moses, saying, "Remove your sandals from off your feet, for the place on which you are standing is holy ground" (Exod. 3:5, MEV). What is the significance of this statement?

Moses is on the back side of a desert, confused about his identity and purpose. I imagine Moses must have been thinking, "Why would God allow me to be raised in the house of Pharaoh just to be banished from the kingdom and then turn around and send me back to lead my people to a kingdom of their own?"

The reality is that God wasn't calling Moses to deliver His people, because He knew Moses didn't know how to do that. As we can see from the passage in Exodus 3, Moses responded to God with misfit excuses, "Who am I that I should go to Pharaoh? Who shall I say sent me? What should I say to them?" (See Exodus 3:11, 13.) He didn't realize that God wasn't looking for a man with a plan already in mind; He just needed a man who would walk with Him. That's why the Creator asked Moses for his shoes, because once Moses let God direct his steps— when he let God get into his shoes—the misfit would be able to do anything God commanded him to do.

We know the rest of the familiar story. Moses went back to Egypt and God sent ten plagues upon the land because Pharaoh refused to let the people of Israel go. Here's where we discover our password, in the last of the ten plagues that came upon the nation of Egypt.

Pharaoh still would not heed God's word through Moses to let God's people go, so God gave him one final warning. The Lord would go through the midst of

Egypt, and all the firstborn of Egypt would die. It was disobedience like Pharaoh's that caused mankind to be kept from accessing the tree of life, and it was through Moses's obedience that the password was given to regain access to the tree of life. The password: Passover Lamb.

The Lamb of God

In Exodus 12:1–14 the Creator revealed the secret of Passover that would give mankind access to the tree of life and keep death from the Israelites' homes. The instructions were:

- Every house takes for itself a lamb (Exod. 12:3).

- The lamb shall be a male without blemish (Exod. 12:5).

- The lamb must be kept in the house for three days (Exod. 12:6).

- The lamb must be killed (Exod. 12:6).

- The blood of the lamb must be placed on the two side posts and upper doorpost of the house (Exod. 12:7).

God told Moses, "This day shall be a memorial to you, and you shall keep it as a feast to the LORD. Throughout your generations you shall keep it a feast by an eternal ordinance" (Exod. 12:14, MEV). This is such a significant picture of the way to the tree of life that God ordered the children of Israel to observe this day as a feast every year. This one act of obedience kept every house that was covered in the blood of the Passover lamb protected from the death that went through Egypt.

The whole reason God got in Moses's shoes was to reveal to God's people, who were in Egyptian bondage, what brings salvation. The institution of Passover was not the way, but it was a temporary password granting God's misfit people the blessed life while they were living in bondage. What does this mean for you and me in the twenty-first century?

Many of us are living in Egypt under cruel bondage, banished from Eden with no sense of purpose and confused about the very reason for our existence. But God is calling our name, asking for our shoes as He did with Moses, and He wants to introduce us to the Passover Lamb. If we will heed His call and accept the invitation to walk with Him in obedience, the Lamb will lead us back to the garden, where we will eat from the tree of life.

Since the days of Moses, all of Israel had been awaiting the promised Messiah who would redeem them completely. Then a rumor spread that a wild-eyed misfit prophet was preaching by the Jordan River. Soon the people of Israel were going to hear John the Baptist declare that the time for Eden to be restored was at hand, but it would require them to change the way they think. For years they had been taught a system of religion where man approached God through rituals, but a Messiah was coming to restore that broken relationship between God and man.

John's message for months was, "Repent, for the kingdom of heaven is at hand" (Matt. 3:2, MEV). God would move upon John daily, preparing him and the people for the arrival of the Messiah. Everyone thought of the Messiah as someone who would restore Israel as a superpower among the nations, causing it to dominate militarily, and then reign as king. It seems they forgot the prophecies in Isaiah 53 describing the Messiah as a suffering servant who would give His life as a ransom for many. So when the day came for Jesus to be introduced to the world as the Messiah, John did not say, "Behold, the Lion of the tribe of Judah, the King of kings and Lord of lords." His introduction was, "Behold! The Lamb of God who takes away the sin of the world!" (John 1:29).

John was declaring that the Passover Lamb, the ultimate sacrifice for sins, was on the scene to grant mankind a place before the throne of God again. And that was exactly how it was. Jesus came and lived among us to show how God truly felt about mankind. We are accepted, forgiven, justified, adopted, and have been given full access to God's presence! Jesus Christ is the Lamb of God, whose blood allows us to return to the garden of God's pleasure.

The time of temporary access to Eden is over. Sin may have banished Adam from the garden of intimate communion with God, but an ultimate sacrifice has been made, giving us access now. We no longer have to wander through life as misfits who have no reason for our existence. We can again fellowship with God and hear Him give us clear direction, because the system of sacrifice introduced in the garden and then reestablished by Moses in Egypt has been made complete through the death and resurrection of Jesus Christ.

The apostle Paul declared Jesus to be the Passover Lamb who was sacrificed for us (1 Cor. 5:7). But can we be sure that Jesus truly was our Passover Lamb? Consider the following:

- According to the instructions in Exodus 12:1–14, each *house* had to have a lamb in order for death to pass over. In Acts 16:31, Paul and Silas told a prison guard the way to life, saying, "Believe in the Lord Jesus Christ, and you and *your household* will be saved" (MEV, emphasis added).

- The lamb had to be a male without blemish. First Peter 1:18–19 says that we have been redeemed out of sin, not with corruptible things such as silver and gold, but with the precious blood of the Messiah, as *a lamb without blemish or defect.*

- The lamb had to be in the house for three days. Our Lamb was *in the tomb for three days.*

- The lamb had to be killed. Jesus Christ *was killed* by Roman crucifixion.

- God had to see the blood of the lamb on the door of the house. Interestingly enough, Jesus is the Lamb but also the door. He said, "I am the door. If anyone enters through Me, he will be saved" (John 10:9, MEV).

Jesus is our Passover Lamb. He not only protects us from death but also paid the penalty for Adam's disobedience, granting us access to God's presence. Do you need further proof that Jesus is our access to the garden? Paul told the church in Ephesus, "But now in Christ Jesus you who were formerly far away have been brought near by the blood of Christ" (Eph. 2:13, MEV). Before Christ we were misfits, strangers, having no hope and without God in this world.

When Paul addressed the believers in Rome, he delivered a message declaring mankind's justification, which gave him permission to again access to the tree of life. Paul said, "Therefore, as through one man's [Adam's] offense judgment came to all men, resulting in condemnation [banishment from the garden], even so through one Man's [Jesus Christ's] righteous act the free gift came to all men, resulting in justification of life" (Rom. 5:18).

NEW IDENTIFICATION

There is something more that you must know before we navigate through the principles in this book. Not only did Jesus become the Passover Lamb without spot or wrinkle, but He gave us His identity, which gives us the benefit of unhindered fellowship with the Creator. We must address the issue of identity in this book because so many people are struggling to find it.

When Adam and Eve were banished from Eden, they didn't just lose access to God's presence, they no longer understood their purpose. This was one of the casualties of the Fall. Our sense of purpose and identity became marred because of sin and our tendency to stray from the truth of God's Word. This is why we struggle like misfits to know who we are and why we were born. We try to find our identity in our gifts and talents, yet we couldn't be gifted enough to earn access back to Eden. We try to find identity in our economic status, but there is no material price that can buy it. The reality is that Jesus was the perfect sacrifice and He alone gives us a perfect identity.

We cannot look to ourselves for acceptance in the presence of a holy God. We must depend upon our access to His identity rather than relying on our own. Those who have known religion all of their lives may have a hard time accepting what I am about to say because religion teaches us to examine ourselves to see if we are acceptable. Paul spent time talking to the believers in Rome about this same situation. But the truth is this: you cannot come to God on your own merit, "For all have sinned and come short of the glory of God" (Rom. 3:23, MEV). The verse makes it clear—we have fallen short.

Religion teaches us to try our best to please God and hope all goes well. This strategy offers no hope for success because the Bible makes it clear that "those who are in the flesh cannot please God" (Rom. 8:8, mev). In other words, we cannot please God in our own strength.

The late pastor and Bible teacher Myles Munroe gave us a great definition of religion in his book *Rediscovering the Kingdom*. He wrote, "Religion is man's attempt to respond to his desire to find some type of meaningful, and possibly intimate, relationship with a Supreme Being as he seeks to find some reasonable meaning to life."[1] As much as we might wish it would guarantee us good standing with God, religion does the opposite. It continually drives a wedge between us and the Creator because it relentlessly shows us the faults in our lives, thus preventing us from drawing close to God on the basis of our goodness. Instead of allowing us to have intimate fellowship with a loving Father, religion causes us to see Him as distant and perhaps disappointed in us because His goodness so far surpasses our own.

One thing religion tries to keep us from understanding is the teaching of reconciliation. The apostle Paul wrote: "For if while we were enemies, we were reconciled to God by the death of His Son, how much more, being reconciled, shall we be saved by His life. Furthermore, we also rejoice in God through our Lord Jesus Christ, through whom we have now received reconciliation" (Rom. 5:10–11, mev). There is another theological term used for *reconciliation*; it's *atonement*. I cherish this word atonement because it helps clarify the value of the finished work of Jesus Christ through the Cross and His resurrection. The account of Jesus's death, burial, and resurrection is not just a good story to hear in church a few times a year; it created a new reality that we need to walk in daily.

Atonement literally means that you and God become one through Jesus Christ. The identity of sin, shame, and failure you had as a misfit is lost as you become one with the spotless Lamb of God, the King of kings. Jesus's blood is enough to make you acceptable before God. He took your place when He died on the cross; your sins were nailed with Him to that tree. Jesus was punished so that you could be forgiven. He was wounded that you might be healed. He died that you may live. He became the curse that you may receive the blessing. Jesus endured your poverty that you could have His abundance. He suffered your rejection that you could be accepted. You didn't deserve it, but He did it for one reason: God wants you back at the center of His garden of pleasure, no longer a misfit but ruling as a king.

YOUR IDENTITY IS SECURE

How do we walk in this reality daily? We must live by the same message that John the Baptist came preaching: "repent." We must change the way we think in order to access the secret place God designed for us to live in. Receive your identity of righteousness before God so that you can walk in the garden fully understanding who you are and what God has called you to do. Quit wondering if you are accepted by God and accept His free gift of righteousness.

Righteousness simply means to be in right standing with God. You have been placed in a position before God where you are fully accepted, approved, and loved by God. You don't have to live in fear, guilt, or condemnation when approaching God's throne. When you receive Christ as your Passover Lamb, you are given His righteousness. It doesn't come by how good or bad you are. This gift of righteousness is given as a promise from God, by the grace of God, and through your faith.

Your faith in His promise brings about your righteousness. This is confirmed in Romans 4:16: "Therefore the promise comes through faith, so that it might be by grace, that the promise would be certain to all" (MEV). For some of you this is a hard pill to swallow, but you must realize that your righteousness before God has nothing to do with you. It depends solely upon your faith in the Lamb of God. So once again, I join with John the Baptist and declare to you, "Behold the Lamb of God!"

This is just the foundation that God is going to use to build you up to be the man or woman He has called you to be. You are about to learn the principles that have led many mighty men and women to do great things in the name of God. These people were not confused about their identity, and they knew what God had called them to do. They experienced life on purpose and to the fullest. In the remainder of this book, I want to teach some principles of how to walk in the garden of God's pleasure. It is in the secret place of intimacy with God that purpose is born and doors of destiny are opened.

Misfits don't become kings when they live to be seen before men or follow the world's rules for success. Rather, our identity, destiny, and success are determined only one way—by what we do in secret.

CHAPTER 4

PUBLIC SIGNS THAT LEAD TO SECRET ENCOUNTERS

I grew up in a traditional Pentecostal pastor's home in the beautiful, tree-crowded mountains of West Virginia. My father is a Spirit-filled minister who has a powerful anointing on his life and a gift for healing. It was not unusual to see something supernatural happen in his services. I have been privileged to see God move so mightily through him that cataracts came off people's eyes as he wiped their faces with his handkerchief. I once stood at the bedside of someone dying in the intensive care unit as my father prepared to read the last rights, and God instead breathed life into the person's dead body.

From a young age, I knew what a powerful, anointed service was like, because I had the opportunity to see the miracles and power of God demonstrated through people who believed God to do the supernatural. I grew up hearing the stories of Smith Wigglesworth, Lester

Sumrall, Kathryn Kuhlman, and other great revivalists from previous generations. I knew the power of God was real because I had seen it firsthand.

Yet as amazing as these encounters were, they were part of my parents' experience with God, not my own personal encounter. This is typical for children who grow up in Spirit-filled homes. It's easy to practice our parents' religion and yet be unsure of what we believe. I see the same thing happening throughout the body of Christ. God moves at church, but something different is happening at home. We are supernatural people in church, but we become normal at home. Everyone loves the experience of God in corporate worship, but not a lot of people have personal encounters with God in private.

I call this the "Psalm 103:7 Syndrome." In this verse, the psalmist tells us that Moses had a personal relationship with God, but Israel stood off in the distance merely watching what God did. The scripture actually reads, "He made known His ways to Moses, His acts to the people of Israel" (MEV). Someone who is intimate with God not only sees what He is doing but also understands why He is doing it. If you stand on the outside and never come close to God for encounters you will certainly see His hand. But Moses did more than that. Moses spoke to God face-to-face.

Do you want God's hand only, or would you like to experience His face? It was this question that provoked me to study the life of the man who talked with God face-to-face, like a man with his friend. Moses walked with God. Despite his own view of himself as a stutterer, ex-murderer, and sheep caretaker, Moses responded to God's invitation for a personal relationship. It was out of this personal relationship that God caused him to rise above the excuses and failures of his misfit ideas and do mighty things in his lifetime.

CREATED FOR ENCOUNTERS

God's original intent for mankind is to walk in constant fellowship with Him. The Lord wants you to encounter Him intimately. He doesn't want you to have just a moment of prayer on Sunday mornings or an emotional experience when you hear someone's testimony. He wants you to have your own personal experience that leads you into an intimate relationship with the Creator. Throughout Scripture you will find the Lord working through circumstances to give people an opportunity to encounter Him.

Moses was a Hebrew who was miraculously rescued from genocide and raised in the house of Pharaoh. He was considered Egyptian royalty and was trained to be great in Egypt. Yet after one zealous moment, Moses found himself on the back side of the desert, watching sheep. It was during his normal routine of tending sheep that he saw a bush begin to burn.

Many of us think of a burning bush as a supernatural phenomenon, but that's because most of us aren't familiar with desert life. The heat of the desert makes it possible for a bush to catch fire. However, Moses began to pay more attention because though a burning bush was normal in the desert, the fire was not consuming this bush. The bush got Moses's attention, but God's intention was not for this bush to be a public spectacle. Rather, He it wanted it to be an invitation to an intimate encounter.

Moses recognized that something was happening and said in Exodus 3:3, "I will now turn aside and see this great sight, why the bush is not burnt" (MEV). Notice the terminology Moses uses in the text: "I will turn aside." Moses was turning away from every other distraction and placing his complete focus on what was happening in front of him. It was in that moment, when Moses drew closer to this supernatural sign, that God took the opportunity to speak. This is a principle spoken of in James 4:8, which says, "Draw near to God, and He will draw near to you" (MEV).

In Exodus 3:4 the Bible says, "When the LORD saw that he turned aside to see, God called to him from out of the midst of the bush and said, 'Moses, Moses'" (MEV). This is the longing of my heart—to be close enough to the Lord that I can hear Him call me by name. It is one thing for an acquaintance to acknowledge you, but it's an entirely different thing when someone of great importance calls you by name. That is what Moses experienced—the most important person in the universe was calling his name.

When God spoke to Moses, He didn't instantly tell him that his assignment was to deliver Israel. God first called him by name. This is true for us as well. Before you are called to do something for the Lord, you must hear Him calling you by name. God was more interested in getting Moses's attention and finding out whether he would spend time with Him than He was in giving Moses an assignment. If Moses had ignored God's invitation to intimacy, would he have received the assignment? The answer is no. You can't tell someone to do something unless that person takes the time to listen to you. The purpose of this encounter was not for Moses to receive an assignment but for him to develop intimacy with God.

Moses took the time to turn aside and behold this supernatural sight. When you take time to turn aside, God will speak to you. But you must turn aside and create a place where God can speak. How many times has God tried to speak to you through circumstances in life but you wouldn't turn aside to see what He was trying to say? God is not interested in anything from you except an intimate relationship.

LOVERS, NOT MERE LABORERS

In their pursuit of having large ministries in America, I believe many preachers have given people a false impression of what God is looking for in those He calls to serve Him. Too often we in ministry portray ourselves to the world as laborers for God instead of lovers of God. In reality, the only reason we are laborers for God is because we were lovers of God first. God wants lovers, not mere laborers.

Lovers will always outwork laborers. A laborer works for a paycheck. A lover is motivated by the relationship.

A laborer will clock out at 5:00 p.m. A lover will work until the job is done in hopes of pleasing the object of his affection. A laborer works hard only for promotion. A lover works hard in order to capture the attention of the one for whom he is working.

This is the secret of those who have done mighty things for God. They weren't merely laborers. Their love for God motivated them to take risks and be obedient to the Lord's every command. Moses was a lover of God. Had it not been for his radical, personal encounter with the Lord through a burning bush, the stories of history would be a lot different.

Even after Moses had spent many years being the great leader and prophet to the nation of Israel, he still did not work for God simply because he was in a position of leadership. His work was motivated by his love for God's presence. Even when God was upset with the children of Israel and was going to have Moses lead the people into the Promised Land without His presence, Moses said, "If Your Presence does not go with us, do not bring us up from here" (Exod. 33:15, MEV).

Moses wasn't interested in just fulfilling an assignment. Moses wanted to make sure that his personal relationship with God was unhindered. In essence what Moses was saying was, "I am not Your employee. I am in relationship with You. The Promised Land is not my goal; my heart is to be wherever You are, God." That should be our pursuit—"Wherever You are, God; that's where I want to be."

God offered Moses the opportunity to inherit the Promised Land, yet Moses said he would not go unless God went with him. He preferred the presence of God over the promise of God. How many people have traded the promises of God in Scripture for an encounter with God's presence in secret? The reality is that the principles of God's Word work because Isaiah 55:11 declares, "So shall My word be that goes forth from My mouth; it shall not return to Me void, but it shall accomplish that which I please, and it shall prosper in the thing for which I sent it" (MEV). If God spoke it, the principle would work even if a heathen applied it, because it's God's Word. But what good would it be to start out with God's presence moving all around you and then find yourself exactly where you have always wanted to be but without the presence of the One who got you there?

How many pastors today are ministering to thousands of people every week but are miserable because the presence of God is no longer in their lives? They remember the days when they had just a handful of people yet their relationship with God was vibrant. They may not realize it, but they have traded the promise for His presence. Instead of scheduling time to host the presence of God as the priest of that church, they administrate themselves away from the anointing.

How many businesspeople are sitting in million-dollar high-rises with money in the bank and several offices across the country and yet are unfulfilled? They started with an idea that God gave them in prayer, but now prayer is a fleeting thought because they are busy maintaining the promise and have no time for maintaining God's presence. Here's the sad reality: if you don't have His presence your promise will only be as good as your ability to maintain it. But if you have the presence of God, you don't have to worry about maintaining the promise in your own strength, because God will empower you to steward the blessings He provides. The arm of the flesh cannot sustain what began in the presence of God.

I'm not trying to motivate you to pursue a great work for God. I'm calling you back to the heart of God, to pursue an intimate relationship with the lover of your soul. You cannot rely upon yourself to fulfill the assignment God has for your life. God wants "co-laborers." He is not interested in watching you work. He wants to work with you and in you. He wants to share His secrets with you and walk you through the process of fulfilling your assignment in the earth. But to have this kind of relationship, you have to learn to seek Him in the secret place. Only His presence can cause a misfit to operate as a king.

SERVICE-BASED CHRISTIANITY

I remember hearing people joke as they locked the church doors, "No saving until next Sunday." But behind every joke is a bit of truth, because we would wait for the next service to see God move. It was as if people only believed God when they were in a corporate church service. And if we really wanted to see God move, we'd wait anxiously for spring revival or summer camp meeting.

People waited all week to come to church just to pray. We couldn't just pray on the streets for someone to get saved. We had to invite the person to church so he or she could get the full experience of what it meant to be a Christian.

We also believed that God would do certain things in services only when particular people were around. For instance, God could only release healing when the healing evangelist came to town. Somewhere in our service-based Christianity we lost our true identity in Christ. We attributed every move of God to a building and certain individuals. We didn't realize we were seeing the power of the Holy Spirit moving through a person who was intimate with God.

Back then, we just enjoyed the show, and the people being used of God didn't mind us watching them. However, we are in a new day, and this generation is not satisfied with watching God work through others. They are hungry to know the secret that leads to being used by God. There is a cry in this generation's heart for the supernatural. But if we only lead them to the supernatural, our assignment is not yet complete.

Throughout the Book of Exodus we see a sad reality at work that is a perfect reflection of what is currently happening in the body of Christ. The people of Israel were satisfied with Moses encountering the face of God on their behalf. Many people who go to church operate the same way. They aren't willing to take the time to ascend the mountain of God in prayer and Bible study. They want the pastor to have a relationship with God and communicate with Him on their behalf. This is not what God wants for His children.

True love relationships are intimate and personal. How would your marriage work if you communicated with your spouse only through a third party? How would your dating relationship work if you sent someone else to spend time with the person you were interested in? You would stay single, and the other person would steal the individual's heart. God was inviting all the people of Israel into His presence when He called them a nation of priests (Exod. 19:6), because priests minister to the Lord and host His presence. But the Israelites chose instead to serve God through another man's relationship.

How sad it is to know some people today who call themselves Christians will only be able to tell other people's stories of God's work in their lives and never have their own because they wouldn't take the risk to spend intimate time with their heavenly Father. You can't afford to be only a spectator of God's presence. Just as Moses did, go as far as you can to encounter the true and living God!

SIGNS POINTING TO GOD'S HEART

The burning bush was a supernatural sign. But it was not put there to become a spectacle. The sign was pointing to a greater reality. I grew up in a time of spectator Christianity, when we watched signs and wonders take place in services as men and women were used of God. We cheered them on, and lived off their revelation and anointing instead of our own personal walks with God. People loved being in the presence of God during services, but they would get in the car with nothing changed in their mind-set, marriage, or lifestyle. They had joy in the service but no peace in their hearts.

We learned how to "do church" but not how to walk in a personal, intimate relationship with God. We were like the children of Israel who knew the acts of God while Moses understood His ways (Ps. 103:7). The children of Israel recognized God's power, but Moses knew His heart. I've been saved for many years and I know the power of God, but I'm just now discovering His heart.

It is so sad when I find people who can talk about the miracles they have seen but who have experienced such an identity crisis that they have backslidden many times and have become unsure they are in a right relationship with Jesus. When I was growing up, ministers with good intentions often preached about exterior things, such as how we dress, how often we attend church, and how frequently we pray. Yet we never got to the root. We didn't realize that behind the traditions was an invitation to a relationship with God. So a generation became misplaced.

Mankind was created to walk with God in secret, intimate fellowship, away from the noise even of organs, shouting, and bold preaching. When I was attending church growing up, we knew how to shout with a booming voice, but we couldn't recognize the still, small voice that changes our soul. We can't depend on external power encounters to keep someone in a vital relationship with the Lord.

Many people have seen the power of God and yet have walked away from Him countless times. Just look at the disciples. After three-and-a-half years of seeing miracles and watching Christ's ministry, when Jesus the Shepherd was struck (crucified on the cross), the flock scattered. They ran for their lives. But once they knew the heart of God in redemption, nothing—not even death itself—could back them into a corner, as we see again and again in the Book of Acts. Miracles alone do not produce love for God. Only encountering God's love causes someone to remain in an intimate relationship with Jesus Christ.

A NEW BREED OF SEEKERS

God is raising up a new generation in this hour that is hungry for the genuine power of God. They are not satisfied with our church routines, outdated media, and cheesy advertisements. Nor will they settle for how God used to move through His people. They want to know God—His heart, His ways, His power—and how He will use them to change the world.

I don't want to waste your time giving you methods simply gleaned from other men and women who were used by God. I want to show you why God used these intimate lovers. God used them because they learned how to "do it in secret." They had a secret life with God that caused them to be elevated above the traditions of church to display the glorious power of the Holy Spirit to a misfit people who forgot that their original purpose was to be in fellowship with their God. The power of God is not here only to mesmerize us, but rather to draw us into the loving heart of God.

You may not have seen a burning bush on your way to work last week, but God is still sending "signs," and they are there for one reason. It's not to point us to a church building, a preacher, or denomination. It's to point us in the right direction, which is to a loving God who gave us His Son and Spirit that we might walk in intimate fellowship with Him. You have an invitation into God's presence. Answer the call today by following the signs that lead to the secret place and there you will find how God turns misfits into kings.

CHAPTER 5

SECRET PRAYER, PUBLIC SHADOWS

Since the beginning of time, people have been trying to answer the question, "Why am I here?" It's the question of every misfit. They want to know if this life really matters and what is the point of living. There are many spiritual and scientific reasons for our existence, but I do not intend to present you with a bunch of theories. I believe this question is answered clearly and simply in God's Word.

Revelation 4:11 says, "You [God] have created all things, and by Your will they exist and were created" (MEV). You and I were created for the will of God. We were not created to try to find our way through life like blind men looking for water in a desert. There is a good, acceptable, and perfect will of God for each and every individual who has ever been created. And God is longing to use each person as part of His redemptive plan to reconcile the world to Himself. The problem is that the space between our ears called the brain has to be renewed in order for us to find God's will.

The secret of God's will, purpose, and destiny for your life is not far off. It can be found in the greatest gift mankind has ever been given: the Word of God. The Author of life and creation left us sixty-six books of instructions, stories, examples, and revelation that can guide us through all the different seasons of life. But you must make a conscious decision to dig into His Word in order to renew your mind and find His will for your life.

God has placed deep inside your spirit a purpose that only you can fulfill. Because of the fall of man and the temptations of life, this purpose is rarely found because few will take the time to walk through the Word and the hidden chambers of their heart to uncover the mystery of their purpose and destiny. So you must ask yourself, "Am I willing to submit my misfit self to the process of knowing God in order to know my purpose?"

Daniel 11:32 says, "The people who know their God shall be strong, and carry out great exploits." If you grew up in church you have certainly heard this verse over the years. But what if I told you there was more to this verse than meets the eye? The Book of Daniel was originally written in Aramaic. When you look back on the original language, the verse would be better translated this way: "but the people who know their God intimately will know their reason for existence." In other words, your identity, purpose, and destiny are locked up in pursuing an intimate relationship with the Creator.

I've heard it said that the more you know about God the more you will learn about yourself. I believe this to be true because we were created in the image and likeness of God (Gen. 1:26). Throughout the Scriptures, you will continually find writers encouraging us to grow in the knowledge of God (Eph. 1:17; 2 Pet. 3:18). Why? Because God's characteristics and nature are in our spiritual DNA. Second Peter 1:3-4 puts it this way: "His divine power has given to us all things that pertain to life and godliness through the knowledge of Him who has called us by His own glory and excellence, by which He has given to us exceedingly great and precious promises, so that through these things you might become partakers of the divine nature and escape the corruption that is in the world through lust" (MEV).

Satan's world system wants you to think that there is nothing different about you. Satan wants you to fit into his system. But when you get to know God through His Word, you will begin to awaken to your divine nature and realize that the reason you are a misfit is because you were created to be a king in His plan, not ordinary in Satan's.

I want you to be awakened to the divine nature that is in you. Sin and pointless religion want you to believe that God is not involved in the affairs of this life and that we must wait until we die to experience heaven. No! If you walk in intimate fellowship with Jesus Christ, you can walk in the power of heaven here on this earth now. You were born for more, and that divine nature is longing to be awakened in you so you will know that the Garden of Eden experience is still available to those who will spend time walking in their reason for existence.

When I use the term *divine nature*, I am talking about the real you that God placed deep inside your spirit but that may be trapped under a heart that has become hardened by life experiences. Your divine nature is the person God made you to be apart from the sin of this world. Every ability, gift, intuition, and talent comes from this nature. This nature can only be unlocked to its full potential when you engage the Creator through His Word and in prayer. These are two non-negotiable disciplines that lead to the activation of your divine nature, which will reveal the reason for your existence.

You may be asking, "How do I walk with God intimately?" That is a question that I hope to answer with a verse the Lord gave me when I was first called into ministry: "He who dwells in the secret place of the Most High shall abide under the shadow of the Almighty" (Ps. 91:1). What an inviting scripture! Though penned thousands of years ago, it still catches the attention of seeking hearts. It will provoke something inside those who will take time to meditate on it. This verse has spoken to me through different seasons of life, and yet it still has the same effect on me now as it did the first time I read it. It produces in me a desire for an intimate walk with the Lord.

THE SECRET PLACE

Often people don't find intimacy with God naturally. In most cases, the secret place of intimacy with God is found during very difficult seasons in life. It was no different for the great deliverer and prophet Moses. He had been through a very difficult time with the children of Israel, and God was tired of the Israelites' attitude and constant complaining. So, desperate for intimacy with God, Moses pleaded, "Please, show me Your glory" (Exod. 33:18).

God responded to His humble servant by saying, "Indeed, there is a place by Me. You must stand on the rock. While My glory passes by, I will put you in a cleft of the rock and will cover you with My hand while I pass by" (Exod. 33:21–22, MEV). It was following this powerful encounter with the Lord that Moses began to write about the secret place of the Most High.

I love the phrase God inspired Moses to use concerning this meeting place for God and man. *The secret place.* This is the invitation back to the Garden of Eden, the place of God's pleasure. The phrase "the secret place" is not used much again in Scripture except notably in the New Testament when Jesus said, "But you, when you pray, go into your room, and when you have shut the door, pray to your Father who is in the secret place; and your Father who sees in secret will reward you openly" (Matt. 6:6). If you want to develop intimacy with God, you need a secret place, a place where you can shut the door and spend some time with your heavenly Father.

This is the starting block of returning to Eden and learning how to be intimate with God again. The secret place is where instructions are given, wisdom is supplied, deliverance is released, healing is received, and the grace is released for misfits to become the person God has created us to be. To "do it in secret" is to learn to walk closely with God privately so that you can unlock your full destiny publicly.

I wonder how many have settled for a mediocre misfit life, barely accomplishing the purpose for their existence because they did not learn to find the secret place. Only heaven knows; but if you walk intimately with God in the secret place, you can know beyond the shadow of a doubt that you lived your life to the fullness of God's potential.

SHUT THE DOOR

The absolute hardest part of having a secret life with God is not allowing ourselves to be distracted by other things. In a technologically driven world, distractions are constant. It's normal to get phone calls, text messages, e-mails, app updates, and calendar reminders all at the same time. It's normal nowadays to have headphones in your ear, a laptop open on the desk, the phone by your side, and friends all around you.

Distractions are part of life today, so for many the idea of being alone in a room with God, whom we cannot see, seems far-fetched. Yet the men and women who have shaken the world are those who found a place of solitude with God. I was praying one day and asked the Lord, "Where are the men and women who shake entire nations with the power of God?" God responded, "They will again, once they quiet down enough to hear the Voice who formed the nations!" Shut the door and become one of those voices who shake nations!

The distractions today may be normal for us, but they are unprecedented compared with previous generations. Our Bibles are on our smartphones. If this is the case, maybe you should put your phone on airplane mode while you are in the secret place. Otherwise, while you are reading a passage of Scripture that is speaking to your soul, a text message from your friend will pop up, and you will be derailed from meeting with the Creator of the universe.

Just imagine with me for a moment that you are in the Oval Office with the president of the United States of America. The president leans toward you and begins sharing his heart concerning a very important issue, and you get a text message. Without hesitation, you reach into your pocket and begin texting a reply to your friend. What kind of response do you think you would receive from the president when you returned to the conversation? Not a very pleasant one. Yet we do this to the ruler of all things created, who gave Himself as the sacrificial lamb for our sins. We need to wake up and realize that God is not a mystical being. He is a person who longs for fellowship with His people.

Once you get the door shut to your secret place, you have won half the battle. Then you must realize that once the door is shut, you are in the very presence of God. You are not alone, according to Matthew 6:6, but the Father is in the secret place. It's time to learn how to walk with God as Adam did in Eden, enjoying unhindered fellowship with your Creator. I mentioned that shutting the door is half the battle; the next step is learning how to stay in the secret place.

ABIDING IN THE VINE

The second word from Psalm 91:1 that I want to focus on is *abide*. The original Hebrew word is *luwn*, and it means to dwell, lodge, pass the night, and to cause to rest. This doesn't sound like a fast-paced, big-city-style prayer life. It's a "take your shoes off and stay awhile" kind of prayer life, as we would describe it where I'm from in the hills of West Virginia. Don't get in a hurry when it comes to the secret place.

Many of us have going to the secret place down pat. We meet regularly with God, present our wish list to Him, and then get up from the place of prayer forgetting that God wants to talk back. Andrew Murray, the nineteenth century author and pastor, said, "Prayer is not monologue but dialogue; God's voice in response to mine is its most essential part."[1] In most cases we do a great job of hammering out our needs before God's throne, but not a good job of waiting to hear God's response.

After all, is not our greatest desire to hear His voice? When God speaks, worlds are created. Yet we think our many words in the secret place are going to change the world. What changes the world is when someone on earth gets God to open His mouth and communicate back, because if God speaks you know you have been heard and His creative force is backing up what He just told you.

Many may be thinking, "But I don't know how to hear God's voice." Don't make it too difficult. I believe God speaks audibly, through visions and dreams, and through other people. But sometimes the loudest His voice will get in your life is through His Word. I tell the people I pastor that I can teach them how to hear from God every day. With much skepticism many wait for my solution, and then I will say, "Read the Word of God until He speaks!"

Many people read a certain number of chapters each day, and I think any type of consumption of the Word of God is great. But if you want to hear His voice, read the Word until He speaks. And then when He speaks, take it all in. Meditate on what He is saying and when necessary, "dig a well." That's a phrase I use to mean "study it out." God may show you one brief passage of Scripture that brings life to you. But if you feel a stirring in your spirit that there is more, don't just close the pages. Dig a well.

If you are reading a verse about the love of God and you receive revelation about a certain portion of the text, look up the verses that are cross-referenced and go to websites such as Blue Letter Bible to see how each word in the verse is defined in the original language. Learn to mine the text for gems. This is a part of learning to abide in God. We leave the secret place too quickly, most of the time without hearing His voice.

Jesus speaks of abiding in John 15:7–8. He said, "If you abide in Me, and My words abide in you, you will ask what you desire, and it shall be done for you. By this My Father is glorified, that you bear much fruit; so you will be My disciples." This is such an important passage, especially at a time when many people believe that anyone who operates in spiritual gifts is automatically one of Christ's disciples.

Here again, we see the opportunity: "*if* you will abide in Me." This means not only abiding in prayer and experiencing the presence of God, but also abiding in God's Word. If you will begin to abide in God's Word, your desires will begin to align with His desire for your life and what you ask in prayer shall be done. This is a powerful truth concerning answered prayer that I think we often miss.

In the context of John 15, Jesus is speaking of people who are His disciples. Jesus is the vine, the Father is the vinedresser, and we are branches. This means that we should have no desire but to produce what is in the vine. A branch doesn't get to determine what it will produce; it produces what it generated from the vine.

The Father watches to see how the branches are doing and determines if the branch can be left alone or needs to be trimmed back. So the vine produces the life (or fruit), and the vinedresser determines what actions need to be taken for the branch to yield maximum fruitfulness. For some reason this does not fit well into most Westernized views on prayer, because we have been taught that God answering prayers is God doing what we ask Him to do.

James, the brother of Jesus, gives us a very precise look at this concept. So many people get frustrated in prayer because they are not seeing results. It's because their time in secret is focused on what they want instead of on what God wants to do with the needs they just presented to Him. James said it best: "You ask, and do not receive, because you ask amiss, that you may spend it on your passions" (James 4:3, MEV). James is saying that if you aren't seeing results, it may be because you are asking selfishly and not according to the desires of the Vine you are connected to. You are to desire what the Vine desires.

Let's go a little deeper with this thought. John the Beloved wrote a powerful word in 1 John 5:14–15. He said, "This is the confidence that we have in Him, that if we ask anything according to His will, He hears us. So if we know that He hears whatever we ask, we know that we have whatever we asked of Him" (MEV).

John the Beloved was the most intimate follower of Jesus, and it would be appropriate for him to pen this passage of Scripture. John is telling us that we can have confidence in prayer when we learn to ask or desire things that align with God's will. But how will we know His will if we don't learn to abide in His Word?

We need a fruitful generation who learns to abide in the vine. We have certainly had gifted generations in the church, but it doesn't help the cause of the kingdom for people to simply be gifted; they must have fruit to back up their gifts. How many times have we seen great men and women of God fall publicly? Too many mighty men and women of God have fallen in these days. For some, their sin was a shock because of how powerful their gift was. But behind the scenes, when history unfolds, we will see that they forgot that they were just a branch. They tried to grow their own thing and rely upon their gift. But a gift will take you where only fruit can keep you. I will prove that to you with a passage from the Gospel of Matthew.

Jesus said, "Therefore by their fruits you will know them. Not everyone who says to Me, 'Lord, Lord' shall enter the kingdom of heaven, but he who does the will of My Father in heaven. Many will say to Me in that day, 'Lord, Lord, have we not prophesied in Your name, cast out demons in Your name, and done many wonders in Your name?' And then I will declare to them, 'I never knew you; depart from Me, you who practice lawlessness!'" (Matt. 7:20–23).

This is probably the scariest verse in the entire Bible. There will be people on the Day of Judgment who will stand before God and say, "I operated in the gifts You gave to me and in the power of Your name." But He will say, "I never knew you." The Greek word translated *knew* means to know intimately. So this verse is telling us that Jesus will say to them on that day, "You used My name and My gifts to accomplish mighty things, but you didn't take time to abide in Me."

As I was praying one day over this passage from Matthew 7, the Lord spoke so clearly into my spirit and said, "The gifts of the Spirit prove that I can use a man, but the fruit of the Spirit prove that I can change a man." The truth of Matthew 7 became so concrete in my spirit in that moment. People become so deceived by those who are gifted, thinking their gift is the anointing or even that God's power somehow validates the person's behavior, even if it's bad.

This will be how the elect are deceived in the last days because false christs, false prophets, and even the false prophet and the Antichrist will be able to perform lying signs and wonders. That's why Matthew 7:20 starts by saying Jesus's disciples will be known by the fruit they bear. You can fake power, but you cannot fake fruit.

My prayer is that you will respond to the invitation to the secret place and learn to abide in Jesus and His Word, because then you will be fruitful. A fruitful generation abiding in the Word will not fall away when put in public view because they are connected so deeply to the Vine. We must pray for those who have fallen, that they will once again learn to abide in the vine, because the fruit is what glorifies God and qualifies us as disciples.

THE SHADOW

While meditating on Psalm 91:1, I came across a phrase I will never forget: "under the shadow of the Almighty." In prayer one day, God spoke softly to my spirit and said, "Not only can you abide under My shadow, but you can carry it." Any time I receive an impression in my spirit, I always compare what I hear to the written Word of God. So I searched through the Scriptures and I found Acts 5:14–15: "Believers were increasingly added to the Lord, crowds of both men and women, so that they even brought the sick out into the streets and placed them on beds and mats, that at least the shadow of Peter passing by might touch some of them" (MEV).

As I read this passage I couldn't help but notice that people were not waiting for Peter to lay hands on their sick. They just wanted Peter's shadow to pass over them. That's when I knew the Holy Spirit was showing me something. I thought, "This shadow cannot be what we think of as a shadow. It must have a deeper meaning." And it does.

The word *shadow* used in Acts 5:15 can actually mean an "aura" radiating off an object. We all know that Peter was a man who sought to know God in the secret place. Many times in Scripture he is on his way to the temple to pray. Peter was not carrying a mystical aura around him. It was the tangible presence of God, the shadow of the Almighty that was resting upon him.

Peter had found a secret place and learned to abide there under the shadow of the Almighty. When you learn to abide under the shadow, you will begin to carry the shadow of the Almighty. The people in Acts chapter 5 were not being healed because of the shadow of the *sun*, but because of a man who carried the shadow of the *Son*. When you begin to carry the shadow of the

Almighty, which is the tangible presence of God upon your life, things begin to happen.

At the beginning of my walk with the Lord I devoured the Word of God and books on revival. One of the first books ever given to me was one on the life of Smith Wigglesworth titled *The Power of Faith*. After I read that book, I began devouring any and every book I could get on this man. I read that Smith once got into a trolley cart with a Catholic priest, and without Smith opening his mouth the convicting power of God came upon the priest. When I read that story, I began to believe from that moment on that I would one day carry that type of anointing upon my life, where people could tangibly feel God's presence on my life. I wanted to learn how to carry the shadow of the Almighty.

In June of 2010 I launched into a new phase of my life where I was traveling in itinerant ministry. The very first revival meetings the Lord gave to me were in Newberry, South Carolina, at a Pentecostal Holiness church. As I was preparing for the services, I prayed for the presence of God to be tangibly expressed through my life. I didn't want the services to revolve around my sermons; I wanted people to have a genuine encounter with God's presence.

It was the very first service on that Sunday morning. I was walking down one of the outside aisles, and as I approached the middle section a woman began to cry. Throughout the service the woman became more and more broken. At the end of the message I gave an altar invitation, and the lady who had been crying was one of the first ones to respond.

Following the service, I approached this lady because I was interested in what the Lord had done in her life. When she began to talk I was taken aback by her British accent because we were in a small town in South Carolina. The lady proceeded to tell me that she was from London but was in South Carolina visiting family. She had been an atheist for years and only came to church because she wanted to spend time with her family.

She thought it would be nothing—just a few songs and a quick sermon, and out the door she would go. But she said when I passed by her at the beginning of the service, she felt a tangible presence come over her body and heard a voice whisper to her, "Everything this young man will say this morning is truth. Listen to him." That morning I shared the gospel, and she responded not because of my message but because of the presence of God that was upon my life. Since that day I have believed for more testimonies of God's presence drawing people, not only by the preaching but by experiencing the tangible presence of God.

My prayer for you as you read this book is that you will find a secret place with God. You need a place to get alone with Him. You need to get away from the noise of the culture to hear the voice that formed and fashioned the universe. Take God's holy Word and learn to abide in Him. God doesn't mind you talking, as long as you remember that He wants to talk back. Then as you begin to experience what it means to dwell under the shadow of the Almighty, I pray that you would also begin to carry the shadow of His presence with you everywhere you go. Go into the secret place and spend time with God, because those who pray in secret will begin to see they are "fit" to carry public shadows.

CHAPTER 6

MAKING A PRIVATE APPOINTMENT FOR PUBLIC INFLUENCE

I n this generation a facade of success is being painted. We measure success by the opinions and approval of human beings. We live to be popular. With the evil called "the pride of life" raging inside us, we long to be seen and heard. We base our success as individuals on how many "likes" we get on Facebook, how many followers we have on Twitter, and how many hearts we get on Instagram. Simply put, we measure our success by the approval of man.

God never designed you to find your approval in man; He wants you to receive your approval from Him, your Creator. We live stressed and complicated misfit lives because we are living for the wrong praise. We once again must renew our minds and find our source of strength from a secret life with God. The Bible says, "The fear of man brings a snare, but whoever puts his trust in the LORD will be safe" (Prov. 29:25, MEV). We can either fight the rest of our lives trying to win man's acceptance, or we can be safe in the arms of God's pleasure.

The fear of man has destroyed the faith of millions throughout human history. If we are going to learn how to "rule as kings" we must find our fulfillment and approval in the One who dwells in secret. As believers in the King of kings, our desire must solely be to please Him. In God's kingdom, the only opinion that matters is the King's. We do not have to strive to be people pleasers because our approval does not come from them.

When our delight is in pleasing the Father, our fulfillment will come through obedience to what He has commanded. His approval is all that matters! We must separate ourselves from those who bend to peer pressure, political correctness, and popularity. We live not for an audience of this world; we live for an audience of one. We are committed to the only King of kings and Lord of lords! No other opinion should matter. If we have become faithful to Him, we will find ourselves safe from seeking the approval of others. Their words will no longer control our destiny and keep us bound to a misfit identity.

I once heard it said, "If you live for the praises of men, you die by their criticism." How true this statement is. When we don't trust God as the source of our approval, we find ourselves unguarded from man's criticism. When we allow man's opinions to give us our sense of worth, we give people power over us that should belong to God alone. Then their words become the fuel for our success or our failures. Don't you want to find your fuel in the One Romans 8:28 says makes all things work together for your good?

The enemy of your soul knows how powerful the opinion of man is, and that is why he tempts us through the lust of the flesh, the lust of the eye, and the pride of life. Our adversary knows that we have to compromise certain truths of God's Word in order to win in the eyes of this world. I believe one of the greatest sins of my generation is that Christians compromise being fully pleasing to God in order to obtain public popularity. When we do this, it only reveals that we seek the approval of this world and not God.

I am only sharing this because it's hard to "do it in secret" when your longing is to be successful in public. In the kingdom we measure success by how obedient we are to God in private. The natural response to private obedience in the kingdom is public influence. So the end goal of a believer is not public success; it is public influence. But God will not entrust us with public influence until we prove ourselves obedient and find our identity in the One who dwells in the secret place.

This will be the major fight for anyone who wants to make a godly impact upon his or her generation. We in the body of Christ continually see what the world calls success, and we try to translate that into the life of a believer. But with that mentality we end up messing it all up. We do not need to look at the world to find success; we must look to the One who was fully pleasing to the Father: Jesus Christ.

PROVE IT

Prove it. This is what many of us have struggled with from the time we are children. We fight to prove to everyone around us that we are something. Or perhaps we struggle to prove that we aren't something. From the time we faced the fear of peer pressure in school, most of us have been out to prove ourselves, and it only continued into adulthood as we tried to advance in our careers. The culture we live in says we have to prove who we are in public in order to validate our identity.

If you are a strong person, it wouldn't matter if you had twenty-two-inch biceps; you would have to do something to prove you are strong. It's not good enough today to know the facts about yourself; you must be able to prove to others that what you know as truth is true. This, I believe, is the reason we have so many people making idiotic decisions in order to prove who they are, even when it's not who they are. The fear of man is a trap, and most of us have fallen into it on multiple occasions.

In John's account of the life of Christ, we find Jesus, like a misfit walking in Galilee away from the Jews in Judea because they sought to kill Him. Jesus's brothers were standing by and told Him to go into Judea because the people needed to see the works He was doing. The brothers said, "For no one does anything in secret, while he himself seeks to be known openly. If You do these things, reveal Yourself to the world" (John 7:4, MEV). This was a call for Jesus to "prove it," to show that He was who He said He was.

This passage of Scripture lets us know that at this point in the life of Christ, Jesus's brothers did not believe in Him. So they gathered around Him and tried to provoke Him to prove something to the world. If He could go out and get a following then they might acknowledge His identity. This is where His brothers were confused. Jesus was not a politician trying to get the people's approval. *Jesus had one assignment, and that was to be fully pleasing to the Father.*

This is where I believe this generation is missing it. God called us when our desire was solely to be intimate with Him, but after a few people started paying attention to us, listening to us, and doors of opportunity started opening, we started worrying about the opinion of man. Soon we found ourselves trying to "prove" ourselves to people whose opinions have nothing to do with our identity. We live in a generation obsessed with likes, comments, and retweets—in other words, the opinions of man—and we wonder why we feel so distant from who we truly are. We remain misfits.

You were not designed to be a people pleaser. If we could just get a revelation concerning our purpose in life, we could understand true liberty. When we live for the opinions of others, we begin to think their opinion is our identity. We are trying to please Jesus's brothers when the reality is there's nothing you can do to truly gain people's approval. If you have it for a moment it will be gone in the next. That's why it's a waste of time to let the opinions of those who don't believe in you shape your identity.

You must have a resolve in your spirit that whatever God has called you to do, whether that is to be a preacher, singer, actress, or business owner, your goal is simply to be fully pleasing to the Father, not to have the most fans or followers. Living for public opinion will cause you great grief in private. So why not do the opposite of what the culture wants? Why not be great in private? If you'll choose to be fully pleasing to God in private, you'll find the courage to be the real you in public without worrying about what other people think.

If you want a life of significance, if you want to do or be something great in this world, if you want to influence people and be the very best you can be, let me save you from years of headaches. Don't build your dream on people's opinions; build it upon what God Almighty has said about you.

How many celebrities or "stars" seem to be truly happy? The only ones I have seen who seem truly happy are the ones who have a sense of purpose and feel they are making a difference by what they do. But those living for fame, fortune, and popularity are on a slippery slope. That's why we see them going in and out of rehab, marrying and remarrying, and doing what's best for business. Unfortunately, these cycles of destructive behavior are only the outward signs of an inward struggle. These misfits are living for the wrong pursuit.

I have a friend named Ricky Scaparo who is the founder of a ministry called End Time Headlines.[1] At the time of this writing, nearly 225,000 people were following his ministry and news updates online and through social media. The response he gets depends on what topic is being discussed. But the feedback doesn't distract him from his God-given purpose, which is to share today's news with a prophetic perspective. His mission is simple and clear cut. People don't always agree with what he shares, because everyone has an opinion not only on the news but also on how it correlates with Scripture. But Ricky doesn't write to please people. If he did, he would never get to fulfill his purpose; because opinions constantly change, he would get nothing done. That's why people's opinions cannot be your source of identity.

The church needs people who will quit looking for how many "likes" they receive on their Facebook updates and instead live to please the One who called them. Paul warned Timothy of this struggle when he said, "Endure hard times as a good soldier of Jesus Christ. No soldier on active duty entangles himself with civilian affairs, that he may please the enlisting officer" (2 Tim. 2:3–4, MEV).

Paul is likening us to soldiers, because anyone who accepts the call of Christ will spend the rest of his days in conflict with the world's way of thinking. You will face hardship in this life, but when you do, don't get tangled up in it. Keep pleasing the One who enlisted you in the fight. Be like Jesus and keep your pursuit pleasing God and not trying to prove yourself in public.

Too many Christians are tangled up in the affairs of this life. They started off with a desire to please God, but now their pursuit has changed. Money has become their focus, and they desire to keep everyone happy. If they will be honest with themselves, they are miserable misfits. When they first started to pursue their calling, they desired to please God and everyone knew they were committed to the Lord. But now they notice a difference. The one who was going to change the world has become just like everyone else. They are tangled.

TANGLED BETWEEN TWO PURSUITS

The tangle is about trying to please God and man, which is impossible. Jesus said, "No one can serve two masters; for either he will hate the one and love the other, or else he will hold [be loyal] to the one and despise the other" (Matt. 6:24, MEV). If you feel yourself torn between pleasing God and man, I encourage you to take a moment to evaluate your calling by answering one simple question: Who called you?

It's so easy to begin to experience success and forget who called you. I can speak from personal experience. I am living in the middle of my God-given purpose right now. When I was eighteen years old, I had an experience with God that radically changed my life. I saw several phases that God would take my life and ministry through. I saw the crowds, connections, and platforms. I saw a hundred acres of land with a gathering place for young people and a youth camp. As a teenager I saw my purpose unfold through the eyes of my spirit.

Less than ten years later, I am living inside of that dream. I currently pastor on one hundred acres of land, and there is a gathering place for young people and we are beginning to plan the development of a youth camp. On top of that, I've had connections that I couldn't have imagined in my wildest dreams. I have preached on major Christian television networks and ministered in some of the greatest churches in America. Yet I will admit that through the majority of this I've had to fight against getting entangled.

People have told me, "You are just young and passionate. You will see that it doesn't take all that to be effective in ministry." Or, "You shouldn't preach on those issues because there are a lot of people who don't see that as a problem." Then I would go back to my hotel room and enter into the tangle of trying not to put man's opinion over God's Word. I don't know how many times I have wrestled with the questions, "What if they are right? Should I just take it easy and preach things that are popular?"

These questions not only began to creep into my ministry, but they caused me to relax my own personal convictions. I'm not saying I started drinking or viewing pornography. I relaxed the intensity of my prayer and devotional life to the point where I was ministering and experiencing "success" without true intimacy with the One who called me. I was in the tangle between acting like a misfit and reigning like a king.

In public I found myself receiving the applause of man, yet in my secret place I felt the sense of compromise because I knew I was no longer pursuing the Lord as I once had. I was so miserable, because I knew I could have more and yet I was fine with settling for less.

LIVING IN LESS

I would preach, and the power of God would move. I watched as God touched people and tears fell from their faces, yet I was unmoved. I was entangled. This eventually led to a season when I began having strong panic attacks and I could hardly be alone. I would not fly in airplanes, and I couldn't go on trips by myself for fear that I would die alone. It was unbelievable at times the amount of fear that entered my life. I was becoming the very thing I told myself I would never be: fake. So, like Job, the things I feared the most came upon me.

I was preaching faith from the platform yet I was privately living in fear. I put on my religious ministry face in public, but I was entangled in every way in private. I couldn't stand what I had become. I was a man who once knew the power of the secret place and was now having to do my best in front of people. I can tell you now that I'm on the other side of fear. The applause of man, being on television, and seeing ministry success could not deliver me from this despair.

I wasn't delivered from the opinions of man in a moment; it was gradual. I made daily decisions to return to the life that made me feel fulfilled. It was the pursuit of Jesus that brought me to a place of influence and fulfilled vision, and I could not settle for less than a wholehearted pursuit. So when I speak of being tangled, I'm not talking about a concept that sounds good; it was something I walked through. I refuse to allow anyone to pursue his or her God-given call and think the pinnacle of success is a crowd applauding their performance. The pinnacle of ministry is to know that you are fully pleasing God in the secret place.

When I first started this project, I wanted to write something that would inspire people and let them know that God is able to bring about His will for their life despite their background, economic situation, or social status. Even though I will show those specific truths in these pages, this book is about so much more than that. I hope it will become a manual for life that people can return to in difficult times so they will keep from getting tangled between the pursuit of public popularity and the pursuit of pleasing God in private.

Time and time again, it is the latter pursuit that has brought ultimate fulfillment to my life. But here is the interesting thing. Pleasing God in private leads to public reward. The question now before you is, Will you be faithful to God in private for the true reward in public? It's up to you how you will "do it in secret." Will you allow your success in life to be determined by popular opinion, or will you allow the Holy Spirit to show you the true success that comes from fully pleasing the Father?

THE SECRET TO SUCCESS

Many people see the highlights of leadership but not the hard work and practices developed in the process of becoming a great leader. People see the lights, camera, popularity, and extraordinary moments of success, but they don't see the hours of preparation it takes to make those moments happen. True success doesn't just happen to someone. Popularity can happen overnight in an Internet-crazed world, but lasting success can come only through discipline and preparation. However, we cannot rely on secular principles to see success; we must rely upon biblical principles as our guide to true kingdom success.

There is a place where misfits become kings, and that is the secret place. Jesus said the secret place is anywhere you can get alone with God (Matt. 6:6). This goes beyond the traditional American church culture where we get everything we need from God in a one-and-a-half-hour service on Sunday morning. In Matthew 6:6, Jesus didn't assume prayer was even an option; He said, *"When you pray..."* He expected people to make an appointment with the Father to spend time with Him in intimate fellowship.

Matthew 6:6 is a part of one of the greatest sermons in the history of the world, the Sermon on the Mount. This is where Jesus laid the foundational teaching for the Christian faith, and He assumes we will pray, fast, and give. These three disciplines are not optional; they are expected to be part of the life of a disciple of Jesus Christ. Success begins in secret.

WHEN DO YOU PRAY?

Many people can tell you when they do something because we are creatures of habit. We like routines and if asked we can usually lay out our schedule for the week. Is prayer part of that routine? Do you set aside time to get alone with God and allow Him to speak with you?

Prayer is an essential part of our walk with God, and we should value it enough to make it a part of our routine. There are so many benefits to prayer, but unfortunately many people don't really see the value in it.

Author and preacher E. M. Bounds once said, "No learning can make up for the failure to pray. No earnestness, no diligence, no study, no gifts will supply its lack."[2] When I meet with the people I pastor, no matter the conversation, situation, or difficulty, we end up coming to this one question: How is your prayer life? I learned very quickly that the most difficult seasons of my life occurred when I allowed the cares of this life to distract me from my relationship with God. When we fail to pray, we keep a closed door on God's direct activity in our lives.

Prayer is the door that allows God to get involved more precisely in the affairs of our lives. Theologian John Wesley famously said, "God does nothing except in response to believing prayer."[3] What I believe John Wesley was saying is that God has placed us in a position of authority but also dependency, and He is waiting for us to invite Him into our every situation to move on our behalf.

Second Chronicles 16:9 says, "For the eyes of the LORD run to and fro throughout the whole earth, to show Himself strong on behalf of those whose heart is loyal to Him." The loyal heart is a praying heart. God is looking for those who are loyal to the secret place, and when He finds them He will show Himself strong on their behalf. When you pray, God gets involved.

When you pray, He removes obstacles. When you pray, He makes impossible situations become possible. That's why I ask, "When do you pray?" Because when you pray He will move!

What promises we have when we pray! In Mark 11:22–24, Jesus said, "Have faith in God. For truly I say to you, whoever says to this mountain, 'Be removed and be thrown into the sea,' and does not doubt in his heart, but believes that what he says will come to pass, he will have whatever he says. Therefore I say to you, whatever things you ask when you pray, believe that you will receive them, and you will have them" (MEV). No matter the situation you can move it by prayer. This is what confounds me with Christians. Why do we not pray?

When we pray:

- Mountains move (Mark 11:23)

- Healing is released (James 5:15)

- Sin is forgiven (2 Chron. 7:14)

- Stress is relieved (Ps. 4:1)

- Anxiety is removed (Phil. 4:6)

This is just a brief list of the benefits of prayer. Really, whatever you need will be provided when you pray. But even if these were the only benefits of prayer, wouldn't your life be much different if you prayed? So as you are scheduling out your time this week, ask yourself, "When am I going to pray?"

WHERE IS YOUR SECRET PLACE?

Don't make this complicated. The secret place doesn't have to be in the same location, but I do have certain places that are for God and me. The easiest place for you could be your bedroom or a spare room in your house. Maybe you have a place on a beautiful mountain that you like to go to. Pick out some places where you can shut out the noise of culture, the distractions of life, and people. You need a quiet place where you can clear your mind, speak the truth from your heart unhindered, and be able to hear His still, small voice.

Choose a place that has a good door. When I speak about a door, I don't mean a physical door. The "door" represents a place of secrecy. God loves our corporate prayer, but He is captivated by the love of one who prays in secret. You need a door between you and the busyness of life. You need a door between you and the negative influences in your life. You need a door between you and church life. You need a place that is not influenced by life and is only focused on Jesus Christ.

There are so many examples of the closed door in the Bible. The first one that comes to mind is 2 Kings 4:1–7, which paints a beautiful picture of intercession. The Bible says that a son of one of the prophets had died, and his widow was left with two boys and an incredible amount of debt. The debt was so high that her sons were facing forced labor and slavery to repay it. This woman knew that the prophet Elisha was in that general area so she went seeking a word from God. This is the first part of this story that I want you to focus on:

no matter where you are or what's going on, what you need to get to the other side of that situation is a word from God.

As the woman was telling Elisha her dire need he asked her a vital question: "What do you have in your house?" Her response was, "Your maidservant has nothing in the house but a jar of oil." Oil always represents the Holy Spirit in or upon the life of a believer. In this passage, the amount of oil the woman had was not enough to meet her need. This is so much like the average believer who has a limited understanding of what it means to have a relationship with God. The initial deposit of "oil" God supplies to a believer can increase as we grow in our obedience to the Word of God and are filled afresh with His Spirit.

Elisha, a prophet under the inspiration of the Holy Spirit, gave the woman a word to obey. Elisha knew the secret to multiplying the oil was more vessels and a closed door. So he was saying in essence, "If you will go and gather empty vessels and bring them behind the closed door, the oil will multiply." I hope you can see the picture begin to unfold.

The widow represents the intercessor who is totally relying upon the Lord (Jesus even used a parable of a widow in Luke 18:1–8 to explain the power of prayer). The widow's need to repay a huge debt represents the situations and obstacles we face. The oil she had represents the Holy Spirit in a person's life, though the widow underestimated what could happen with the oil. Yet as she obeyed the instruction of the prophet of God, the oil multiplied in the vessels her family gathered and was enough to meet their need.

This is what God does to a person who spends time in prayer. You are the empty vessel who is in desperate need of oil, and the oil that multiplies behind a closed door in the secret place is what will help you meet the need you are facing. The vessel seemed like just a normal jar for oil until the door closed and the oil began to pour unhindered. You may be reading this right now and thinking, "I just have a little bit of oil and a lot of needs all around me." Close that door right now in Jesus's name, and cry out for God to increase the oil upon your life. As you begin to spend time in prayer, God will pour upon you blessing, fresh perspective, new direction, health, and ideas that will meet whatever need you are facing. Let the oil multiply behind the closed door. Do it in secret.

PUBLIC REWARD IS PUBLIC INFLUENCE

The promise of Matthew 6:6 was that when the Father sees you in secret He will reward you openly. Everyone loves rewards; we are motivated by them. That is why it is important to realize that the discipline of intimacy with God in secret promises reward. You may be wondering, "What is the public reward?" I believe the public reward is the power of God demonstrated through your life.

This goes back to the story of Moses in Exodus 33:15–16: "Then he said to Him, 'If Your Presence does not go with us, do not bring us up from here. For how will it be known that I have found favor in Your sight, I and Your people? Is it not by Your going with us, so that we will be distinguished, I and Your people, from all the people who are on the face of the earth?'" (MEV).

I don't think there is any greater reward than to know you carry the presence of God in public. That is how Moses viewed the strength of Israel. It was not based upon their earthly possessions but rather on the fact that the presence of God was with them. Because of His presence, every need they had was met. They never went thirsty, hungry, or in want of natural necessities because He was with them.

Many people see the power of God demonstrated in public, but they don't realize that before God rewarded someone in public that person was seeking God in private. Everyone hears about the souls that were saved in public, but they don't hear about the intercessor in secret crying out on his knees for people to be saved. People only see the public manifestations of God, so it's easy to forget that the only reason they are seeing this reward is because someone invested time with God in private.

Even after major revivals, the people most often remembered were the phenomenal preachers who spoke, the singers who worshipped, and those who shared powerful testimonies of God's grace. But what people didn't see were the prayers in private that took place for generations beforehand in communities and prayer closets all over the world. Miracles, revival, awakening, and demonstrations of God's power are birthed out of the intimacy of the lovers of God.

I have heard many people ask mighty men and women of God what their secret to success was. And so many times I have heard the same response: "My relationship with Jesus Christ." One of the most touching moments I have witnessed on TV was when Billy Graham was being interviewed on Fox News.

The news anchor, Greta Van Susteren, asked him, "If you were to do things over again, would you do it differently?" Billy Graham's response was life changing for me. He said, "Yes, I would study more. I would pray more. Travel less. Take less speaking engagements. I took too many of them in too many places around the world. If I had it to do over again, I would spend more time in meditation and prayer and just telling the Lord how much I love Him and adore Him. And I'm looking forward to the time we are going to spend together for eternity."[4]

I'm sure this statement astounded many people, because we value productivity for God over loving God. Even Greta Van Susteren seemed surprised as she asked him why he would want to speak less when he drew such large crowds. But Billy Graham has reached a point in life where he has a great perspective. He realizes the greatest thing in life is to do it in secret—to get alone with God and build that vital relationship.

His heart for prayer and the secret life was so evident by his statements. Many would consider Billy Graham the most successful religious leader of this era. But I think he was letting us know that our reward is God's presence, and the rewards we see in his life are a result of the time he spent with God in secret. That is the place where grace flows to do mighty things for God. Let us learn from this principle of success: the reward in public only comes to those who make an appointment with God in secret.

MAKE AN APPOINTMENT

"Don't pray when you feel like it. Have an appointment with the Lord and keep it. A man is powerful on his knees."[5] Those are words from Corrie ten Boom, author of *The Hiding Place*, and how true they are. When we are dealing with serious issues of life—health, finances, or business challenges—we must make an appointment with the Lord.

We set appointments when a meeting is important and we don't want to miss it. When we schedule an appointment, it becomes "official" in our minds, and that is where we plan to be at that particular time. Why do we schedule appointments with our doctors? Because our health is important. Why would we make an appointment to pray? Because our relationship with God is important.

A great mentor and friend of mine once told me a story of a man who had been saved for more than sixty years and was a pillar in his church. One day this man invited him over to his house for a meeting because he wanted to show him something. The meeting was set for 4:15 p.m., and when my friend arrived, this older gentleman asked if they could take a walk.

The two strolled down a path on the man's property and when they went a little ways down a hill my friend noticed a fire pit with a wooden bench beside it. The man asked my friend, "What do you see?" He told him, "It's an altar." But the man said, "No, it's my meeting place with God. And every day at 4:15 p.m., I have an appointment with God in this very place, and I pray until God speaks to me."

This was the man's secret to successful living. Every day he got off work at 3:30 p.m. It took him thirty-five minutes to get home, and every day when he arrived, just like an official appointment, he met with God at 4:15 p.m. Rain or shine, hot or cold, he had an appointment. My friend said that when this man would pray, you could feel the presence of God. That doesn't surprise me, because God doesn't miss appointments with us.

Do you have an appointment set up with God? If not, set one now and develop a secret place where you can get alone with Him. If you want true success, you must learn the secret, and that is intimacy with God.

CHAPTER 7

DISMANTLING THE
PUBLIC PURSUIT

I t has been said that the kingdom of God is an upside-down kingdom. The truth of the matter is that we are the ones upside down, and the kingdom is right side up. We have been taught about life from a sinful perspective, where success is determined by how much material gain you can amass and how many people you can get to serve you. The kingdom of God, however, is not about material gain at all but about positioning ourselves to be servants of all. What a different way of thinking. We must begin to dismantle worldly paradigms if we want to become fruitful as kings in the kingdom.

As I discussed in an earlier chapter, when Jesus walked the earth even His own brothers had the wrong mentality about success. His brothers thought Jesus was preaching and performing miracles in order to be a public figure. But in all actuality, everything Jesus did was in obedience to what the Father led Him to do in secret. Jesus's brothers had no revelation of Eden or having a secret life with God. They thought Jesus wanted to become a religious or political figure. How sad that Jesus's own brothers thought the whole purpose of following God was to be well known. They failed to realize that Jesus had one pursuit: to walk with God like Adam did in the garden and to be completely obedient to His will.

Jesus said in John 6:38, "For I have come down from heaven, not to do My own will, but the will of Him who sent Me." This one statement alone challenges the very core of our culture. We have been told that we should follow the dream of our hearts and do what's best for ourselves. Everything is centered on pursuing our own will. The model Jesus left for us was to deny our own will and do the will of our heavenly Father.

This is the key to true kingdom success. The Creator has designed each of us for a specific assignment, and He knows where we need to be for maximum impact. We are lost without God's direction; we have no clue where we should be and what we should do. Sure, we can glean from past experiences and make decisions based on trial and error. But God knows exactly where we need to be, when we need to be there, and what we should be doing for maximum impact. Why not trust Him to lead the way?

The only way to experience the fullness of God and make the greatest impact is not by doing what we can think up in our minds. It's by seeing how we can position ourselves to hear God's voice and then respond with joyful obedience to what we hear. That's why the enemy of your soul wants your greatest desire to be public success, because then you will strive in your own ability to get a platform of some kind, whether for ministry, your career, or your personal life.

In the kingdom we must be turned right side up and make our greatest pursuit a secret life with God through which He guides us by His will into maximum impact. After all, we are disciples of Jesus Christ, so we must follow in His ways and submit to His disciplines. The denial of self was one of Christ's elementary principles.

I am going to say that we must dismantle our pursuits, because in order to submit our wills to God we must learn how to wrestle our wills to the cross of Christ. Our will must be continually placed upon the altar of God until the agony of its death gives way to the joy of following God in the garden of His pleasure. It's the greatest exchange in the history of the world, but it often takes some time for our misfit minds to be convinced of that.

This is where a true secret life is built and why it is so important to spend time with God in prayer. Many of us go to God in prayer during times of crisis, but it was designed for so much more. I want with all that is in me to encourage you to pray but not like a hypocrite. Jesus said hypocrites "love to pray standing in the synagogues and on the street corners that they may be seen by men" (Matt. 6:5, MEV). But He adds, "Truly I say to you, they have their reward" (MEV).

Prayer is not a religious thing we do publicly to show the world we believe in God. Prayer is something we do in private that shows God that we trust Him. When prayer becomes public only, it loses its essence. Prayer is not about creating a good image for yourself in front of others. Prayer is about the personal interaction you have with God. It is this private interaction with God that produces a powerful and accurate representation of who God is through His people in public.

We have it backward, and Jesus wants to put prayer back in its rightful place. I do not have a problem with corporate prayer; I participate in that on a weekly basis. However, public prayer should not be our main objective when we are around others. When we are in public, God wants us to represent Him well through the lifestyle that is birthed out of our private and intimate prayer times with God. The only way to have a powerful display of God's power in public is to have powerful prayer in secret.

The religious hypocrites Jesus described in Matthew chapter 6 were praying in public for only one reason: to look good in front of people. But a person who has been with God in secret has a different goal when in public: to help others experience their own personal encounter with a living and relational God.

POLITICAL PRAYERS

How many times have we seen political figures stand and deliver speeches that stir the masses only to turn around and make decisions contrary to what they promised? Why is that? Because many politicians will say whatever it takes to get the votes they need to stay in power. All too often, politicians are not out to do what is best for the people; they want the people to get in line with their agenda. They are often looking to scratch one another's backs, forgetting the very reason they have the position, which is to serve the good of others, not to force their agenda upon the masses.

It's no wonder Jesus had to address this political mentality when teaching on the subject of prayer. Beginning with this hypocritical approach to public prayer, Jesus tore down the religious mind-set of His day. Men would pray in public because it impressed the people. The end goal of public prayer was essentially political. In that religious culture, prayer was seen as commendable, honorable, and popular. These men wanted to use prayer to sway public opinion and control people, not to fellowship with God. Using prayer to this end not only defeats the purpose of prayer, but it belittles our relationship with God.

Imagine for a moment that I talk with my wife only in public, but my goal is not even to talk with her but rather to impress other people by making it seem as though I am communicating with her. Do you think my wife would figure out the shallowness of my relationship with her very quickly? Of course! Why? Because true intimacy with my wife requires sincerity and my undivided attention. Yet this is how many of us treat God. We want to publicly acknowledge God for the sake of appearances, but we avoid the secret place, where God can have our undivided attention. When our relationship is on this level, it is shallow.

When we pray so that people will hear us, our motivation is political at its core. What is politics? It's all about influence and organizing control over people. It is always centered on a person's agenda. At the core of political prayer is the individual, and the aim of their prayer is to be seen. The Bible says the greatest among us is the servant of all (Mark 10:44). But Christians who pray political prayers want people to serve them. Prayer was never supposed to be centered on us or used to advance our agenda. The goal of prayer is to be aligned with the Creator.

It's no wonder that many today are not experiencing true spiritual growth. I want to recommend that before you go public with God you first commit to have a secret life with Him. This is how many have been a bad representation of God in front of the world. We present our idea of who God is, but because we never get close enough to Him to actually know Him, we cannot show the world who He truly is. The only way to represent the true God in public is to get to know Him intimately in the secret place. Too many people have head knowledge of God but not intimate, experiential knowledge of Him. So they lead people to an intellectual conversion rather than a life-altering encounter with a personal God. There is no room for political prayer in the kingdom of God. It's about His will, not ours.

Personal Prayer

Jesus is not a religion, so religious praying will not lead to true spiritual change. Jesus came so we could once again have a relationship with the Creator. Relational, secret prayer is what brings about the right connection. Aren't you tired of fruitless religious practices that exhaust you more than the other cares you have on your plate? When Jesus becomes personal to you, His refreshing presence will remove the burden of religion off your back. Take a risk and get intimate. No more praying because "it's the right thing to do." It's time to get intimate because you are in relationship with God.

I describe prayer as intimacy. Intimacy is a powerful word that I believe explains the essence of what true prayer is. Intimacy means closeness or close familiarity, much like what is shared between a husband and wife. When you are close to someone, you understand things about him or her that other people don't catch. For instance, there are looks that my wife gives that communicate things to me that no one else would understand. Every look represents a different message. I can understand those looks because I'm intimate with my wife. I understand her without the use of words.

The psalmist David found such intimacy with God that he heard God's Holy Spirit say in Psalm 32:8, "I will instruct you and teach you in the way you should go; I will guide you with My eye." Imagine this place of intimacy with God, where words are not used but God's eye is directing you. That type of relationship doesn't happen overnight but takes time to develop through intimacy.

We are not to approach prayer as a mystical thing. Many people think it is mystical because they don't realize that it is actually personal. God is not a blob of mystical light floating in the unknown above the stars. God is a person. The Bible even describes Him with physical features.

- God has eyes (2 Chron. 16:9)

- God has a mouth (Isa. 1:20)

- God has arms (Isa. 59:1)

- God has feet (Exod. 24:10)

- God has nostrils (Exod. 15:8)

- God has ears (Ps. 34:15)

These verses suggest that if God has these features, then He can see, speak, reach, walk, smell, and hear. These are just a few elements of His person, yet they let us know that God has the ability to engage with us personally in much the same way we interact with other people.

It Started With a Chair

For me, personal prayer didn't start at an altar at church. It actually started with a chair in my bedroom. We had just moved into a home on 12th Street in Nitro, West Virginia. I was working at Circuit City at the time and was unavailable to help my family on moving day. To my surprise, when I came home, my parents had given me the master bedroom of the house. It was a nice, spacious room that had more than enough space for my bedroom furniture. But there in the middle of the bedroom was a nice La-Z-Boy chair. It was one of my father's favorite chairs, but he and my mother had given me the spacious room and that nice chair so that I could spend time with God.

Many nights I came home from work and would shut the door and spend hours reading the Word of God and crying out for the Holy Spirit to anoint me with power. It was alone in that room that I learned to hear the voice of God. Did I hear an audible voice? No, but I recognized His way of impressing something in my spirit, and I became sensitive to His leadings.

One thing that has made a lasting impression upon me was when the Lord led me to buy a map of the nations and place it on my bedroom wall. During my prayer times I would place my hand on different sections of that map and pray for God to send me to the nations. The thought of going to nations began to consume my mind as I read about how the disciples took on the world with the gospel of Jesus Christ. I wanted to follow in their footsteps. I felt like I was ready to change the world, but in reality, I didn't even know that I would need a passport to travel outside the United States. I had barely been out of the state of West Virginia, but I knew God was calling me to the nations.

I would place my hand upon Central America and imagine preaching crusades in those countries. Many times my hand would move over Asia, and then like a magnet it would be drawn to India. I could see myself preaching the good news to the masses and altars filled with people accepting Christ. My prayers went from words to seeing His promise in my spirit as God opened the eyes of my understanding.

Then the confirmations began to come. This is where prayer gets fun! Many times God will drop phrases, ideas, impressions, and visions into your heart, giving you glimpses of direction in your pursuit of destiny. Then because you are seeking His will, God will send other praying people to you to confirm what He has already spoken into your life. This is the essence of a prophetic word.

As the call to the nations burned in my soul, different ministers in different church services began to call me out of the crowds and prophesy that I would be a voice to the nations. Then in these moments of confirmation the man or woman of God would say the exact phrases God had placed into my spirit during those times in prayer, confirming to me that we were both hearing from God. This has fueled my prayer life. I love to receive prophetic confirmation in public of what I have heard from God in secret.

With each confirmation came a sense of knowing the will of God. So with every leading it became easier to obey what God was asking me to do. I have found that with every act of obedience, big or small, part of the reward mentioned in Matthew 6:6 is to receive publicly what you asked for privately. Everyone can see the blessing in public, but they won't see the work and sweat you put in prayer to see that thing come to pass. I don't want to give the impression that prayer is not work. There are days when I feel like praying and there are other days when I have to make myself pray. But I have learned that history belongs to those who make room for God in private. Will you be one of those who are determined to make history, or will you continue to pray out of religious duty?

Making a Long-Term Commitment

Too many people make crisis commitments to Christ rather than long-term commitments to know Jesus in every way possible. The apostle Paul described his assignment to preach the gospel by saying, "that I should preach among the Gentiles the unsearchable riches of Christ" (Eph. 3:8). Paul knew the riches of Christ were unsearchable, yet he preached because of what he found in his committed pursuit of God. True intimacy with Christ will never bore you but will provoke you to pursue even more intimate moments.

If Christ's riches are unsearchable, then short-term commitments to prayer will not even begin to scratch the surface. If we really want to enter into the deep things of God, it begins with making a lifelong commitment to search out the unsearchable. After all, true eternal life is about knowing God and Jesus Christ whom He sent (John 17:3). Your greatest privilege now and through all eternity is to pursue the unsearchable riches of Christ.

If the riches of Christ are unsearchable, then accept the invitation to search them out. Don't settle like the hypocrites of Jesus's day with making public prayers just to be seen. When we pray we must go where men cannot see in order to discover what eye has not seen. The only reward you get for public prayer is the impression you make on those watching or listening to you. The hypocrites' treasure was the opinion of man. But the reward of private prayer is receiving the fullness of who God is.

You no longer have to wander around in the dark, uncertain of where and how to pray. You have a treasure map in Matthew chapter 6 that tells you where to find the "X" that marks the spot. But let me encourage you. When you start digging, you will find treasures galore. Don't be satisfied with a few jewels on the surface. If you keep digging, the treasure gets more valuable. I'm ten years into the committed journey of prayer, and I haven't been disappointed yet. Even as I write this book I continue to discover new treasures!

THE KEY THAT UNLOCKS DESTINY

"Dr. Lowery is coming to your father's church." Those were the words God spoke into my spirit one night while I was in prayer, and it was the starting point in my understanding that our intimacy with God is the key that unlocks destiny. So many times we think something major has to happen in order for our destiny to unfold. I have come to realize that it's in those moments when you hear the still, small voice of God that major things begin to happen.

Deep inside each person there is a sense of destiny. It's an inward stirring that causes you to just know that God has predetermined certain things to happen. You may have seen documentaries or interviews where certain individuals said they knew at a very young age that they were "destined" to do a particular thing. Well, according to Scripture we all were born with a specific destiny that was predetermined by God.

Let's take a look at just a few of the verses that speak of God's intended purpose for our lives.

> Declaring the end from the beginning, and from ancient times the things that are not yet done, saying, "My counsel shall stand, and I will do all My good pleasure."
>
> —ISAIAH 46:10, MEV

> For I know the plans that I have for you, says the LORD, plans for peace and not for evil, to give you a future and a hope.
>
> —JEREMIAH 29:11, MEV

> A man's steps are of the LORD; how then can a man understand his own way?
>
> —PROVERBS 20:24

These verses are declaring that God is in control of our lives, that He knows the end from the beginning, and that He has plans to prosper us and order our steps. These verses are wonderful promises, but unfortunately many wander through life never understanding God's purpose or will for them individually. I want you to know today that there is a sure way to make sure you don't miss out on the destiny God has placed inside of you.

Proverbs 25:2 says, "It is the glory of God to conceal a thing, but the honor of kings is to search out a matter" (MEV). This verse has always intrigued me in my pursuit of the things of God. Why would God conceal things? Why would Jesus speak in parables? Why did the prophets use so much symbolism?

While kneeling in prayer one morning, I began to ask the Lord these questions. His response was simple yet profound: "Because I want you to seek Me." The Lord longs for relationship, and in His pursuit of that He will reveal just enough to us to make us want to search for more. Why would God want you to search for Him and to seek out His truth? Jeremiah 29:13 says, "You shall seek Me and find Me, when you shall search for Me with all your heart" (MEV). The Lord loves when His children search for Him because in our pursuit He has our whole heart.

God loves intimacy with His people so much that He will reveal secrets in order to provoke more seeking. But the interesting thing about secrets is that you only share them with your friends. Don't you hear the love language of God calling you into His secret place in order to share with you His mysteries? Moses understood this well. He wrote in Deuteronomy 29:29, "The secret things belong to the LORD our God, but those things which are revealed belong to us and to our children forever" (MEV).

The beauty of searching for God is that when He reveals to you a secret, that knowledge becomes yours forever. One of the things the Lord wants to reveal to you is His perfect will for your life. But you must take the initiative to search Him out, to hear His voice, and to pray for His secrets to be revealed. His secrets will lead you into your ultimate destiny. Everyone's path is different, but the principles of the pursuit remain the same.

So many times in today's culture it seems that we search for our destiny everywhere except in the One who spoke it into existence. I want to give you an example. Let's say you went to the local hardware store and purchased a new high-tech appliance for your home. Upon unpacking the material, the most important piece of information you would have concerning the appliance is the owner's manual. Why is that the most important thing? It's because the owner knows every bit of information concerning this appliance and how it should operate. The owner knows every feature, setting, and way it could malfunction. So three years down the road when something goes haywire or you mess up a certain setting on the appliance, you can just reference the manual and the owner will have the information you need.

If you were to have a problem with your refrigerator, how ridiculous would it be for you to search the manual for the microwave? You wouldn't depend on the owner's manual for the microwave to solve a problem with your refrigerator. Yet this is how we are with God and our lives. We search for instructions concerning our destiny in education, the media, and popular culture, and some even use demonic means such as horoscopes and tarot cards. What we need to do is pick up the owner's manual. God created all of us. He knows our attitudes, emotions, gifts, abilities, strengths, and weaknesses. He knows how to adjust our settings and how to fix our failures. So why do we look any further than His owner's manual, the Bible?

GROUNDED FOR A PURPOSE

After receiving the call of God to preach, I became absolutely obsessed with reading the Word and devouring books on revival. I sought the Lord constantly. I would work my job through the day and then come straight home to study and spend time with the Lord. Then one day I let my guard down and allowed someone of the opposite sex to distract me.

I am not against relationships; in fact, I am happily married with three beautiful children. But in that moment of time, this person was just a distraction. I would love to tell you how consecrated I was to the Lord even after I met this person, but when this person came into my life I got distracted from my intimacy with the Lord. It wasn't that I didn't love God or His Word, but this relationship divided my affection so much that I lost my commitment to the secret place.

Losing that intimate time with the Lord at first seemed like a minor thing until it caused little areas of compromise in my life that led me down a path of dating three other girls though I already knew whom I was supposed to marry. Maybe I was scared to admit that at nineteen years old I knew whom I was supposed to marry and that thought drove me crazy. Was I scared to commit? Maybe so; but my decisions and discernment were off for one reason: I wasn't in the secret place with the One who has all the answers.

The relationships took a toll on my personal devotion to God and on the young people I was preaching to on a consistent basis. They were getting the worst of me because I lacked a vibrant relationship with the Lord. This was a season that I would like to forget. However, it was in that season that I learned the greatest lesson in life: when you lack intimacy with the Lord, you lose your sense of purpose and destiny.

After I dated those three girls, the youth ministry began to grow but not because of the anointing. It was because youth were coming to see what drama would come from that three-ring circus. My father, who was also my pastor, had taken all that he could handle, and at nineteen years old I was given a choice. I could continue in ministry and stop dating and spending time alone with any female for at least a year, or I could keep dating and step down from the ministry.

When my father gave me that choice, my heart sank in my chest. I knew what choice I had to make despite what my flesh wanted to do. Deep inside of me was a call of God, but in those elementary years of following Christ I hadn't quite learned what it meant to "take up my cross and follow Jesus." So at an age when "being grounded" was unheard of, I was "grounded" from dating, and I made a decision to live consecrated to the Lord and His work for the rest of my life.

Looking back on that season of my life I realize I was grounded for a purpose. I found that secret place with the Lord again and even invited friends over for late-night prayer and worship. I moved into the parsonage of my father's church so I could do the work of ministry anytime I wasn't working my secular job. What was once my youth ministry office became my bedroom.

I had a bed on the floor with a desk, television, and Xbox. That was my life of consecration. I would come home from work and study, pray, watch my favorite preachers on DVD, and finish most nights playing a college football video game for relaxation. But I had my secret place back, and I felt His heartbeat again for my generation.

The Lord began to form a dream inside of me concerning what He was going to do through my life. I would pray and see myself preaching in conferences, foreign countries, and churches around the world. I knew that God had called me to be a voice to my generation, and there I was, living in a small church, pastoring fifteen young people at the most.

I quickly became addicted to the presence of God and the work of God. I would fast and pray for those fifteen kids like I was pastoring a megachurch of 15,000. I preached as hard as I do now to those kids back then, because I didn't see fifteen chairs; I saw where God was taking me. Other ministers would come to my father's church who didn't have a clue who I was, and they would call me out of the congregation to prophesy that God would take me to the nations of the world. I was just a little hillbilly from the mountains of West Virginia who thought going to Myrtle Beach, South Carolina, was driving across the country.

I didn't even know what a passport was, so how could I go preach to nations? But as I kept seeking the face of God, He began to move in my life in so many ways I don't have enough pages to share them all with you! In that season of being grounded from dating I learned to be fulfilled by God alone. I know this may sound crazy, but during that time if everyone would have forsaken me, including my family, I would have been just fine because of His presence in my life.

LEARN INTIMACY ON THE JOB

Many people are working jobs that they don't even like. But if they will learn to make that job the training ground for their purpose, God can make time fly by! Many times we miss perfect opportunities for God to teach us lessons that get us qualified for where He is taking us. If we would get alone with God we would realize that where we are is a stepping-stone to God's purpose for our lives. If you will allow God to renew your mind and give you a proper perspective, your attitude would begin to change and you might start enjoying your life.

This is the lesson I had to learn while working at a major technology retail store in West Virginia. I had already accepted the call to minister, but in that season doors to preach were not flinging open, so I needed a job. I will never forget getting hired and management placing me in the infield, which is where I organized the DVDs and CDs and helped people locate the items they were seeking in that section.

This was truly a test of patience, because people do not seem to know how to put products back after they've finished looking at them. I organized these sale items not only alphabetically but also by category. Just as soon as I thought I had gotten everything in place, a family the size of the Duggars would come into my section. I found myself complaining a lot and getting a horrible attitude toward people in general because I knew they just wanted to mess up my section. Then one day the Lord asked me if I thought I was representing Him well in that position.

The Lord gave me a passage of Scripture that gave me a new perspective: "He who is faithful in what is least is faithful also in much. And he who is dishonest in the least is dishonest also in much. So if you have not been faithful in the unrighteous wealth, who will commit to your trust the true riches? And if you have not been faithful in that which is another man's, who will give you that which is your own?" (Luke 16:10–12, MEV). After that point my job as an infield worker went to another level, because I could see through God's Word that He was trying to qualify me for something greater.

I realized that as I cared for the DVDs and treated each customer as one of God's children, I was being prepared for my destiny to lead a generation. I not only came to work with a new attitude, but I knew God was with me, watching how I trained for my future. I was not just organizing CDs anymore; I was being faithful in little because God wanted me to be a ruler over much. Even though it was not my store, I wanted to be faithful over my employer's resources so I could be trusted with my own. You have to know that where you are now is only the training ground of a greater purpose in God.

Because my focus was on being obedient to the passage the Lord showed me from Luke 16, I was promoted to a full-time position in the company three months later. I not only became full-time but the raise I received in my new position was far beyond what other people made who had worked there for years. I continued operating in the revelation God had given me about being faithful, but now I was in need of more grace and favor because the promotion put more responsibility upon me.

I now had to sell a certain amount of product each month to stay qualified for the position. I knew the familiar scriptures about prosperity because I'd heard them preached more than the words of Jesus in red. But as I was praying about the pressure I felt at work, the Lord dropped 1 Thessalonians 5:17 into my spirit and said, "Pray without ceasing." I began to ponder this scripture and its meaning, wondering how it could help me be a good salesman, and then it hit me. God wanted to teach me that He is always with me, leading and guiding me every step of the way. And because He is with me, failure is not an option. Romans 8:31 says, "If God is for us, who can be against us?" (MEV). This became my confidence; I knew that as I kept my mind upon Him, He would lead me by His still, small voice and guide me into the sales I needed.

I didn't know this phrase at the time, but I was learning to practice the presence of God. I was learning how to be intimate with God even while I was on the job and in public. I would pray for God's leading, and my sales numbers would begin to increase. It was like the Holy Spirit would give me the words to say and tell me which direction to go. I earned sales at times when I didn't even know what I was doing, and the managers would have to come out and help me close the sales. The managers didn't mind because the company was making thousands of dollars off these sales.

When my unsaved employers would ask how I was doing it, I would just say, "The Lord is blessing." They would just smile and walk away probably thinking I was crazy. I learned so many valuable lessons during that time that I still live by and that I can share with those who are serving with me in ministry now. If you will learn to be intimate with God where you are, blessings will come and overtake you. So the next time you get ready to complain about your job or what you have to do, remember that it's the training ground God wants to use to bring a misfit into kingship.

BACK TO THE FUTURE

In the Introduction I mentioned an event that has impacted my life to this very moment. It was at Rod Parsley's Dominion Camp Meeting in Columbus, Ohio, in 2006 that I was about to be accelerated into my destiny. It was the last night of the services, and this one was geared toward the youth. It was to be a time of impartation and release of anointing from one generation to another.

In that service Pastor Parsley called three men onto the platform to pray over the young people at the meeting. The first man to grab the microphone was introduced as a former member of the Executive Council of the Church of God, who had a great healing ministry and saw millions of people come to Christ. That man was Dr. T. L. Lowery, a true general of faith to many in the church today.

The second man introduced was Perry Stone, with whom I was kind of familiar because of his Christian TV program, *Manna-Fest*. Then beside him was an older man, Fred Stone, who also was introduced as someone who flows in the gifts of the Spirit and has seen many touched by the power of God. As those three men began to pray over my generation, all I can say is that what felt like a fireball hit my chest and I began to shake under the power of God. It was almost embarrassing because others were just worshipping and enjoying the moment, but I was under the power of God shaking like a leaf.

I was one of thousands in that room that night and had no clue that God was getting ready to connect me to the men on that platform. I wasn't searching for the connection, and even in that intense moment all I could think about was the amazing power of God that was all over me. Not once did it ever cross my mind that I would be connected to Dr. T. L. Lowery, Perry Stone, and Fred Stone. But this is where my life got very interesting.

Several months went by following the camp meeting in Ohio. I was asleep in my bed when my father woke me up and told me about a dream he just had. In the dream my father heard the sound of a service, but the only thing he could see in the dream were two words: *spiritual impartation*. Dad then asked me if I knew what that meant or anyone who was doing that in ministry.

As I sat there and thought about his dream, I remembered that at the camp meeting I saw a banner of Dr. T. L. Lowery with the words "Spiritual Impartation" across the top. When I told him that, my Father said, "Well, let's try to contact him and see what the Lord is doing in his ministry concerning this subject." The next day, Dad called Dr. Lowery's office, but the secretary said he had just stepped out for a meeting. While she was telling us that, Dr. Lowery came walking back in because he had forgotten his car keys. The secretary asked him if he had time to take our call, and he did. The conversation lasted for maybe ten minutes, and during that time Dr. Lowery asked my father to join him in Kingsport, Tennessee, for his Spiritual Impartation conference. This conference was held in March of 2010.

Dad made the journey to Kingsport, Tennessee, and spent three days there in the powerful impartation services. After each service my mother and I called to get updates about what God had done in the meeting. Each time I would ask Dad if he had any time to spend with Dr. Lowery, and the reply was always the same: "He is busy, and we just haven't connected." So I would get off the phone and spend time with the Lord in the secret place.

But one day as I was praying, the Lord spoke to my spirit and told me that Dr. Lowery was coming to my father's church and would ask me to travel with him. In that moment it seemed impossible, but the more I prayed about it the more convinced I became that it was going to happen. Then I got a little bolder and began telling my closest friends what I believed the Lord had spoken to me. I think they all thought I was crazy, but I knew I had heard from God.

When the conference ended, even though my father was deeply blessed by the services, nothing spectacular or unusual happened. A few days after my dad returned from the conference, I decided to tell him what I believed the Lord had said. The very next day, he received a call from Dr. Lowery telling Dad that he wanted to visit our church. When my father asked him when he would like to come, Dr. Lowery said, "This Sunday."

My father was concerned about preparing the church for his visit and placing ads so more people could come. But when he began to share with Dr. Lowery his concerns about being prepared for the services, Dr. Lowery said, "I'm not coming for a crowd. I'm coming on an assignment from God." That's when I knew I'd better get ready, because the first part of what the Lord shared with me was about to come to pass: Dr. Lowery was coming to my father's church. So I knew that I would soon be traveling with him.

I will never forget the moment I met Dr. Lowery for as long as I live. We were in my father's office at our inner-city church in Charleston, West Virginia. When I walked into the room, Dr. Lowery's eyes got as big as silver dollars. He shook my hand and said, "You are the reason I'm here." He said that I was going to be his Elisha and travel the world with him. That was on a Sunday, and by Tuesday I was in Cleveland, Tennessee, at Dr. Lowery's office prepared to follow the man of God.

I spent almost four years traveling with Dr. Lowery and experiencing the power of God. What started as a whisper in the secret place became a reality, because intimacy with God unlocks destiny for you! It's time to change our focus. The public pursuit of success cannot be the center of your life. You should have a burning desire to walk with God in the secret place, where we can abide in His presence.

But intimacy is just the beginning. I believe that once you have developed a secret life with God, He will place you under someone's authority, and that person will cover you and lead you into a greater reality of the plan of God for your life, just as Dr. Lowery and other men of God have done for me. In the next several chapters, we will look at this issue of authority and covering. I dedicate the teaching I will share with you to the men of God who have covered my life and helped lead me to where I am today.

CHAPTER 8

STAYING UNDER COVER

In a generation where we see millions of fatherless homes, leaders without integrity, and politicians who care nothing for the people, it is hard for many to understand true authority. If we have a hard time grasping the idea of authority in the natural, how much more difficult will it be for us to understand true, biblical spiritual authority. In this and the next two chapters I hope to give you a solid definition of what authority is, and how honoring it can benefit your life and put you on the God-track of destiny.

HIDDEN BEHIND A MAN

From the time I was young I carried the idea in my head that great ministers had great mentors. I remember as a five-year-old boy going to the Back to the Bible conference in Charleston, West Virginia, where spiritual giants such as Lester Sumrall, Rod Parsley, and Bishop T. D. Jakes were speaking. I remember hearing Pastor

Parsley talk about his relationship with Lester Sumrall and how it brought a powerful transfer of anointing upon his life. Because of that childhood memory, when I was first called to preach I was compelled to read several books that have shaped my life to this day.

One of the books that left a lasting impact upon my life is *Adventuring with Christ* by Lester Sumrall. Pastor Parsley reprinted the book several years ago, and the Legacy edition he released shares pictures of the two of them traveling together and developing a father-son, mentor-mentee relationship. That book more than any other made me desire to have a spiritual father.

I wanted to be mentored in the things of God. I wanted to learn deep spiritual truths from men and women who have seen the hand of God move. I wanted to glean from those who had an uncompromising devotion to the things of God and were allowing God to move through them to change the world. I was afforded that opportunity after Dr. Lowery came to minister at my father's church.

As I shared in the previous chapter, the transition was quick after his visit, and I was on the road with T. L. Lowery the very next weekend. I was ready and willing to go with him even though I had no clue what was before me. I just knew I wanted to be under the covering of a mighty man of God and was willing to do whatever it took to see a powerful anointing to change my generation come upon me.

Sometimes I think my story is like the account of Elijah and Elisha in 1 and 2 Kings. Their story began in 1 Kings 19.

So he [Elijah] departed from there and found Elisha the son of Shaphat, who was plowing with twelve yoke of oxen before him and he with the twelfth, and Elijah passed by him and threw his cloak on him.

—1 Kings 19:19, mev

Like Elisha, I believe the Lord wanted to take me through a mentoring process before He would allow me to step into public ministry. But I don't think I was a special case. I believe God wants to do this in all of our lives; He wants to take us through a mentoring process to prepare us for where He wants to take us. Your story will be unique, but God will be working behind the scenes every step of the way, connecting you with the people and ministries that can help prepare you for your destiny.

When Elijah first encountered Elisha, he found him working his father's fields. Elisha wasn't just plucking weeds out of a garden; he was plowing with twelve yoke of oxen. This means Elisha was working at least twenty-four oxen in the field at one time. He may have had help in the process, but it doesn't diminish the fact that Elisha was a hard-working person. This leads me to my first point: God will not use lazy people. Anytime you see God calling someone in Scripture, that person is working.

- Moses was tending his father-in-law's sheep.

- Joshua was fighting for Moses and the children of Israel.

- Gideon was threshing wheat.

- David was tending his father's sheep.

- Peter was catching fish.

- Stephen was waiting tables as a deacon.

When I graduated high school, the very first thing I did was find a job. I didn't think college was for me so I began working for a company in retail. I was raised in a family that worked hard. We didn't sit around waiting for something to happen. We were raised to work. I decided to become the best worker the company had, and on my eighteenth birthday I became a manager for the store.

I kept myself busy and enjoyed being productive. Then I was called to preach, but being called to preach and serving as youth pastor of a small church didn't pay the bills. It is amazing to me how many people who are called to do something expect to get paid immediately for what they love to do. Sometimes you have to keep plugging away at a job you don't like until the prophet comes with his mantle.

I felt like Elisha in that season of my life, because though I didn't have twelve yoke of oxen, I had a full-time job, served as a youth pastor, played drums for the church, and went to Bible training courses in the evenings. I was busy doing what I felt God had called me to do and at the same time did what I had to do in order to have finances. I was plowing my oxen when God brought Dr. Lowery into my life.

When Dr. Lowery told me I was to be his Elisha, I had a choice to make. God had a plan to have a mantle placed upon my shoulders, but like Elisha I still had to choose to accept it.

> He left the oxen and ran after Elijah and said, "Please let me kiss my father and mother, and then I will follow you." And he said to him, "Go back, for what have I done to you?"
> —1 KINGS 19:20, MEV

When I was given the opportunity to follow this mighty man of God, choosing to leave home wasn't easy. I had lived in West Virginia all my life. What were my parents going to do without me? How would my friends feel about my leaving? How would the students feel about me leaving them for another opportunity? These were just some of the questions running through my mind, not to mention that I just had proposed to my girlfriend the month before and we were engaged. Would she still want to get married and move to Cleveland, Tennessee, with me?

But I heard from God in the secret place and knew that if God spoke it, He would be responsible for sorting through all of the consequences. God will not lead you into something and not take care of the things that concern you. I remember talking with my father about this transition because it affected him too. Here I was, nineteen years old and deciding to just up and leave my family and all I had known.

There was no promise of a job; I would just be traveling with the man of God. I had never been to Cleveland, Tennessee, a day in my life. I didn't know where I would stay or even fully understand what I would be doing. But I knew I had to be obedient.

> So he [Elisha] returned from following him and took a yoke of oxen and sacrificed them and boiled their flesh with the yokes from the oxen and gave it to the people, and they ate.
>
> —1 KINGS 19:21, MEV

What I absolutely love about Elisha's actions is that they show though he was not going to look back, he wanted to make sure everyone was taken care of before he left. I believe the will of God is that when you leave a place you do everything in your power to make sure it's healthy and better off than it was before you got there. In my case, anyone could have done a better job than I had done as a nineteen-year-old youth pastor. But I made sure the kids were covered, that my friends knew what I was doing, and that my fiancée was willing to make the transition with me.

God moved, and everything came into order just as He had planned for it to. That didn't make the transition perfect, but all the pieces I was most concerned with were handled with great care. I didn't have oxen to slaughter, but there were people I needed to be sure were taken care of before I left.

Then he [Elisha] arose and followed Elijah, and became his servant.

—1 KINGS 19:21

Two days after Dr. Lowery visited our church, I was sitting in his office. I had packed clothes for a few days, but I had no dress clothes to wear. It was quite embarrassing, because T. L. Lowery is one of the classiest dressers you will ever see, and there I was with nothing but blue jeans, black Nike shoes, and T-shirts. But I was determined to follow God's man and become his servant. It was during this time that I began to learn about spiritual authority and that when God wants to do a great work in someone's life He often begins by hiding that person behind another leader.

HIDDEN BEHIND GOD'S AUTHORITY

Whether you are called to full-time ministry as I was or to some other kind of kingdom work, we all need mentors in our lives who can help us navigate through life. This may be a pastor at your church or a small group or Bible study leader, or it may be the person you work for, whether you are in a Christian or secular arena.

The people God gives you as mentors will teach you how to respond to authority. It's important to remember that all authority, Christian and non-Christian, comes from God. The apostle Paul said, "Let every soul be subject to the governing authorities. For there is no authority except from God, and *the authorities that exist are appointed by God.* Therefore whoever resists the authority resists the ordinance of God, and those who resist will bring judgment on themselves" (Rom. 13:1–2, emphasis added).

This may be hard for someone to hear who is under the authority of someone who doesn't treat him well. But even if your situation is difficult, that doesn't mean you are not exactly where you need to be. God knows what leader we need in our lives to prepare us for the destiny He has for us. I have learned through the years that God will even take the bad in leaders to help get the bad out of you now before you become a person of great influence. But we will dive deeper into that issue in a later chapter.

God knows exactly which leaders to put in your life because He knows the end from the beginning (Isa. 46:10). He knows your strengths and weaknesses, the good and the bad. He knew you before you were formed in your mother's womb (Jer. 1:5). God will "hide" you behind someone in order to make you into the person you are called to be. God has many ways of processing us, and if we believe His Word, we know everything will work together for our good!

When God chose the leaders who will have authority over you, He knew their weaknesses and strengths—and those strengths and weaknesses may very well be why He put you together. Like Proverbs 27:17 declares, "As iron sharpens iron, so a man sharpens the countenance of his friend." Sometimes God will bring two hard-heads together to sharpen them!

When I went to work in Dr. Lowery's ministry, I had to learn submission to authority. It wasn't that I was openly rebellious, but I was used to doing things my way as the leader of our church's youth ministry. I learned real quickly that the way I did ministry and the way Dr. Lowery did ministry were very different, and no one was asking for my opinion.

It wasn't about me. This was my learning and serving season. One of the worst mistakes you can make when you are just starting out is to think you know every-thing. You may think you have your hand on the pulse of the culture or that you know the trends in your chosen career field. But you need to have your hand on the pulse of God's heart to know what He wants to do through you. As a young leader serving under someone else's authority, you can offer advice but ultimately you must be willing to submit to that person's authority. If you believe God has ordered your steps and has you working with a certain person for a reason, then know that your destiny is locked up in how well you serve while under that leader's authority.

FOUR SEASONS UNDER AUTHORITY

During my almost four years of traveling with Dr. Lowery, the Lord showed me four seasons of learning I would go through during my time under his authority in ministry. It again parallels Elijah and Elisha, this time from 2 Kings 2:1–15. As we discuss these four seasons, I pray that you will open up your spirit and take the time to evaluate which season you are currently in. Whether you are in ministry or serving under a producer in Hollywood, you will be able to apply these spiritual lessons to your life.

Gilgal: The cutting away of flesh

> Then when the LORD was about to take Elijah up to heaven by a whirlwind, Elijah went with Elisha from Gilgal.
>
> —2 KINGS 2:1, MEV

Gilgal is the first season you will encounter while serving under someone's authority. In Joshua chapter 5, Gilgal is where a new generation of Israelites was circumcised when Joshua assumed leadership after Moses's death. Circumcision is not a popular message, but it is most needed in order for you to get where God is taking you. Circumcision is literally the cutting away of flesh. "Gigal" is the place where you have to learn to let your flesh die. By "flesh," I'm not just talking about our bad behavior and attitudes but also our dreams and ambitions. In this season we are learning to serve someone else's dream. We are helping someone else fulfill his or her vision and purpose in the earth.

This is why we don't see true discipleship in the church today, because we haven't had enough people come through the first season of Gilgal. We have become a selfish generation that does only what we want to do or what benefits us instead of learning the greatest principle Jesus taught: "He who is greatest among you shall be your servant" (Matt. 23:11, MEV). There is power in laying your life down to make someone else's vision come to pass. It was during my Gilgal season that a pastor came to share a powerful principle with me concerning serving another man's vision.

This pastor could tell that I was exhausted from the amount of labor I was providing. He probably could tell that I also was discouraged because, after all, who enjoys dying to self? The pastor told me of a time in his life when he served in another man's ministry. This pastor was determined to serve faithfully. He was dedicated to God and to this man, but he was going through his own Gilgal moment, and he felt underappreciated and that no one else was willing to help. That's when God spoke to him and said, "Every time you are willing to serve this man's vision, while you are serving I'm lining up the people who will one day serve under your ministry."

It was in that moment that I got a second wind for my Gilgal, because I realized that learning to die in this season would bring about life in another season. This struck another chord in me about how I was serving and the attitude I had while doing it. Sometimes it's not just the outward things that need to die in our lives but the inward poison that needs to be dealt with.

After thinking about what the pastor told me, I realized that if God was going to one day have people serve under me when I became a leader, then I wanted to have the best attitude so those serving me later would also serve cheerfully. Whatever you sow, you will also reap; a seed can only reproduce after its own kind. So if you sow a bad attitude while serving, the people you will attract to your ministry or business later will have the same attitude. Make sure you deal with the flesh in Gilgal, because it will determine whom you will attract to your life later.

We cannot escape the Gilgal season, so my question is this: Are you willing to submit to the "cutting away" God has ordained for you? God doesn't put you under someone's authority just so you can hear what you want to believe about yourself. God wants to bring people into your life who will challenge and correct you when you are wrong.

Your mentor may not be a Christian, especially if your calling is in a secular arena. That's why it's important that you connect yourself with spiritual mentors who know the mind of God through His Word and can speak into your life. Sometimes the person being used to help you grow in your calling is your spiritual mentor, which was the case with me. But if it's not, I'd encourage you to pray that God will bring someone (or some ones) into your life who will get to know you for who you really are—not just the good stuff, but the good, the bad, and the ugly. Allowing someone to speak into your life about the good and the bad may not be easy for you, but it will produce major results in your walk with God. If you develop a healthy relationship with the right spiritual authority, that person can help lead you into personal success.

Sometimes you just need someone to talk to. The Bible says in James 5:16, "Confess your faults to one another and pray for one another, that you may be healed" (MEV). Healing comes through confession, and a safe place for confession should be with a spiritual mentor in your life. This may be your pastor, small group leader, or possibly someone you work with, but you need an outlet to share what you are going through. God will use these relationships to help you unite with your mentor's vision on a heart level.

The season of Gilgal isn't easy, but it's crucial. We can't sidestep or avoid it. In fact, the first command we are given when we choose to follow Christ reflects the season of Gilgal. Jesus said, "If anyone desires to come after Me, let him deny himself, and take up his cross daily, and follow Me" (Luke 9:23). Greatness begins in us when we allow God to take away the flesh that is holding us captive from a greater purpose. God brings mentors and authority figures into our lives to help prepare us for greatness later. But selfishness, jealousy, pride, and envy will keep us from accepting the more challenging things those individuals may have to say.

Gilgal is not only a place of circumcision, but the actual name *Gilgal* means "to roll away." In Joshua 5:9 God spoke to Joshua after their circumcision and said, "This day I have rolled away the reproach [the shame] of Egypt from you." This means that while you are in this season God does not want to cut on you out of enjoyment, but He is using the authority figures He has placed in your life to remove the things (shame, disappointments, setbacks, failures) that hindered you previously.

Cutting away the flesh only hurts for a moment, but the joy of being free from the past lasts for eternity.

Bethel: The house of God

The second season you will encounter while serving under someone's authority is Bethel. Bethel means "the house of God." No matter what area you are serving in, you need to be connected to the house of God. Psalm 92:13 says, "Those that are planted in the house of the LORD shall flourish in the courts of our God" (MEV). This is a principle we cannot afford to overlook. Even if we are in business or education, we must find a place to serve in the house of God.

Now, I'm not saying everyone should get a microphone and be in platform ministry. You may need to find the toilet brush or vacuum. The church needs people who are willing to serve. Even King David said he would rather be a doorkeeper in the house of God than dwell in the tents of the wicked. David loved the presence of God so much that if need be he would be a doorkeeper in order to be near His Lord.

When I think of serving in the house of God, I can't help but to think of Obed-Edom in 2 Samuel 6:10. David tried to bring the ark of the covenant back to Jerusalem, but because of someone's ignorance about how to carry the ark, someone got killed. So David, in fear of angering God, kept the ark in the house of Obed-Edom.

Obed-Edom means "the servant who honors God in the right way." Rabbinical literature also tells us that while the ark was in Obed-Edom's home, he would light a candle to it twice a day, once in the morning and once in the evening. This was an act of worship in order to host the presence of God properly.

Obed-Edom's willingness to serve in the presence of God caused his whole household to be blessed. It is the same way when we are willing to serve in the house of God. Even if you are busy with work, find time to let your pastor know that you are willing to serve when you are available. This is a key that most people overlook. I truly believe that when you take care of God's house He will take care of yours.

Because Obed-Edom knew the power of serving before the presence of God, when the ark of the covenant was moved back to David's tabernacle he became a servant in the tabernacle. In 1 Chronicles 15:16–21, Obed-Edom volunteers as a singer. In 1 Chronicles 15:24, Obed-Edom volunteers as a doorkeeper. And in 1 Chronicles 16:5 and 38, Obed-Edom is a minister before the ark.

Obed-Edom saw what hosting the presence of God could do in his home, so he decided to serve in the house of God so the blessing would remain upon him and his family. Being involved in a vibrant community of God's people, willing to serve in God's house, is part of the process that is preparing you for your destiny. I often tell the young people at our church that if they are not willing to serve in this ministry then they shouldn't expect to have a place of influence in the ministry. Jesus calls servant-leaders, not leaders who expect only to be served.

That's how God processed me before I was called to preach. My father had just planted a church in St. Albans, West Virginia, and all the Lord would tell me was to be willing to serve. I fell in love with the presence of God, so I did everything I knew I could do. I played drums for the worship team, cleaned the church, painted the church, swept the sidewalks of the church, and did whatever else needed to be done. I had a heart that was willing to serve.

Oddly enough, I was called to preach while shoveling snow on the sidewalks of the church during a service. I have the same mind-set even to this day, because servanthood is not something you learn in a season, pay your dues, and then move on. It is the attitude you should have at all times, because promotion comes to those who serve.

Jericho: Acceleration of growth

The third season you will encounter while serving under someone's authority is Jericho. Jericho was well known for its fertile soil, which allowed it to have wheat-covered plains and to reap early harvests.

Gilgal and Bethel will get the soil of your heart right. Gilgal breaks your pride and selfish ambition, and teaches you to walk the crucified life, and Bethel teaches you how to have a servant's heart. When you learn to do those two things, you will become fruitful, which is exactly what Jesus wants you to become. He said, "You did not choose Me, but I chose you, and appointed you, that you should go and bear fruit, and that your fruit should remain" (John 15:16, MEV).

Jericho is an exciting season because it is when you begin to see growth in your life. In this season you start seeing the life of Christ mature in you, and your character begins to shine. The wrong attitudes you had are now being transformed into proper perspective. You aren't serving because you have to; you are now serving because you want to please Father God. Whatever you do, you do it "heartily, as for the Lord and not for men" (Col. 3:23, MEV).

This became a reality to me over time as I performed a consistent assignment for Dr. Lowery. When I was working for his ministry, one of the things I had to do was to prepare the sanctuary for services and conferences. We had eight hundred chairs in the sanctuary, and before I made friends in Cleveland I would have to set them all up by myself. There were many times when quitting was an option while moving those chairs, but I persevered, and now I believe I actually have a chair-moving anointing!

Over time, however, whether I was alone moving chairs or had help, I found myself spending time with the Lord. Some of my greatest revelations came during those chair-moving times. This is what I believe Jericho is—it's about accelerated growth. While others are out there trying to start something on their own, because you are under the authority God has given you, you have several benefits:

- You are in God's order, which brings favor upon your life.

- You are being prepared for the vision God has given you.

- Your character is being developed in a place where no one can see it.

- You can learn from someone else's mistakes instead of learning the hard way by yourself.

This is the problem I see with many young men and women who have a call of God on their life. They go out and try to start something on their own and end up beat up and disappointed. But if we follow God's order of being under authority then we will see success. Joshua was powerful because he served under Moses. Elisha was powerful because he served under Elijah. Timothy was powerful because he served under the apostle Paul. Acceleration happens in your life when you place yourself under God's given authority.

Not only do you get to serve and learn, but you are able to glean from your mentor's wisdom and insight. So many people say to me, "Mark, you have wisdom beyond your years." I believe that's because I spend time in prayer and in God's Word. But I also believe it's because I was willing to sit at the feet of Dr. Lowery, who had been in ministry for more than sixty-six years when I worked with him. I gleaned from every story and example he shared with me, and I know that accelerated the growth of my knowledge of ministry and the things of God. You accelerate your growth through the learning you get from your leader.

I want to challenge you to find someone to mentor you. Learn from that person and serve him or her, and I promise that you will grow much faster than someone who has a dream he is not willing to submit to God's order. God's desire has always been to put fathers with sons or mothers with daughters, so one generation can prepare the next to continue to build the kingdom. Throughout the Word of God you can see the Lord using this order to prepare someone for influence.

Jordan: To descend or to decline

This is the last of the four seasons you will encounter while serving under authority. This season can be the most difficult because with the acceleration of growth comes the resurrection of dreams that you allowed to die in Gilgal. When we first come to serve under a mentor, God often will ask us to lay down all our ambitions in order to fulfill the dream of the person we are serving. But in this last season, God begins to resurrect those dreams that He placed in us. We begin to start dreaming of our own ministry, business, or position while still serving someone else's vision.

In Jordan we begin to see how we would do things compared to the person we are serving. It's in this season that Satan tries to get you to turn against the person because of the flaws you see, but Satan always has a ploy to keep you from your destiny. He wants you to turn against the man or woman you are serving to keep you from the impartation you are about to receive. Remember, no matter how great the person is whom you are serving, he or she is just a person. That leader is operating out of what he knows to do, but you will begin to see what kind of leader you are going to be by that person's successes and failures.

It's going to happen. At some point you are going to see the dirt in your leader's life. I'm not necessarily talking about sin. I'm talking about the way he or she manages situations. You will learn how things should and shouldn't be done.

The word Jordan means to "descend," or be humble, and you have to be careful in this season to do exactly that. You must stay humble through this season, because you are bursting with vision and ready to do your own thing. You are ready to move into your own assignment, but that is the test. Are you willing to remain humble even when you have a better idea? Are you willing to remain "low" even when you know you could leave? It's in these moments that God sees if you learned your lessons in Gilgal, Bethel, and Jericho. My advice to you in this season is to not just see the person, but to serve the anointing on the person. Even an unsaved mentor has God-given strengths and abilities that have led to his or her success in that field. If you are faithful to serve the person in Jordan, at the end of the season you will receive an impartation like Elijah gave Elisha.

God desires that His people be humble, not just to advance to the next level, but to become more like Christ. The Bible speaks frequently of our need to humble ourselves:

The fear of the LORD is the instruction of wisdom,
and before honor is humility.
—PROVERBS 15:33, MEV

Therefore whoever humbles himself like this little
child is greatest in the kingdom of heaven.
—MATTHEW 18:4, MEV

Humble yourselves under the mighty hand of
God, that He may exalt you in due time.
—1 PETER 5:6, MEV

As I came to the final season of my journey with Dr.
Lowery, I realized that humility was the key in this
season. Humility, I believe, is when you know you have
something powerful inside of you and yet choose to
prefer someone else above yourself. When you get to
this season of Jordan, you are experiencing the growth
of Jericho. You are in a place where God is birthing powerful things inside of you. But it's still not time for you
to step out and walk in your vision. It has to become
evident to those leading you that you are ready to step
out on your own. Until then, stay humble, descend, and
pass the test of Jordan.

It was in this season that Dr. Lowery began to notice
my gift of preaching and ministry. He began utilizing
me in his services and conferences, and I became a reg-
ular speaker at his events. It was evident to him that
the call of God was upon my life. Yet I still had to be
willing to go back to the office on Monday and stuff
envelopes for mail-outs. That was my Monday through
Friday assignment at Dr. Lowery's. I was the shipping

manager for the T. L. Lowery Global Foundation. This was one of the many ways I passed the Jordan test. I had the ability to preach and minister, yet I was still willing to go in that back office of the T. L. Lowery ministry center and seal envelopes. Just because you have the gift to do something doesn't mean it's time for you to start your own thing.

I believe that if you are humble in Jordan, God will make it obvious when it's time to transition into what God has for you next. That's how it was for me. When I was on the road with Dr. Lowery, people would prophesy over me about my next season right in front of Dr. Lowery. People started connecting with the ministry God had given me in Cleveland, Tennessee (more about that in a later chapter), and it began to grow exponentially. It was obvious that I was pregnant with destiny, and Dr. Lowery took notice.

Moving to the next phase of ministry wasn't an easy transition for me because I absolutely loved Dr. Lowery, and I was comfortable working for him. He is a true man of God and was an excellent leader in my life and family. I honor him to this day for the investment he made in my life. When I sensed the release to go, we both knew it was time for the next season.

I want to encourage you today as you are evaluating your life to find someone to whom you can submit for a season of preparation, someone you can trust to offer leadership during this season of preparation. The person you think would be ideal may not be the one God has for you, so seek God in prayer, and ask Him to connect you with the person He has purposed to mentor you in this season of preparation. Be faithful to that person even if you see dirt in his life. Many times the dirt you see in him will keep you from allowing the same dirt into your own life. But even if the leader has flaws, the gold that is in him will rub off on you as well!

Learn to surrender your dreams and stay humble. At the end of those four seasons an impartation will be released that will carry you into your future, because you will have clearly grown spiritually and/or in your professional gifts. These four seasons are done in secret under the covering of leadership. But if you pass the test, what was done in secret will be rewarded in public.

Today I am happy to tell you that when I minister, the anointing of T. L. Lowery begins to shine through. At times my wife will tell me that I remind her of Dr. Lowery when I minister. I like hearing that because it is proof that the four seasons impacted my life to the degree that now I operate as his son in the faith, which is the order of God.

This is a small revelation of double portion, because I have my portion and his upon my life! Thank God for authority, because I believe I am where I am today because of these four seasons!

CHAPTER 9

DONKEYS THAT LEAD TO DESTINY

Now the donkeys of Kish, the father of Saul, were lost. And Kish said to his son Saul, 'Take now one of the servants with you, and arise, go find the donkeys'" (1 Sam. 9:3, MEV).

It's amazing how God will use someone else's problem to lead you to your assignment as king. It was this way for Saul, who became Israel's first king. I can relate to Saul. His father had an issue with lost donkeys, and my dad couldn't keep a youth pastor. Either way, it's a principle I believe the Bible shows clearly, especially in the lives of Joshua and Elisha.

Joel 2:28 tells us that God will pour out His Spirit on all flesh and that our sons and daughters will prophesy. The prophecy goes on to say, "Your old men shall dream dreams, your young men shall see visions." I read that verse one day, and the Holy Spirit spoke clearly to me, "In the last days you will see a convergence of generations.

The key that will unlock young men's visions is their willingness to serve the older men's dreams."

I am convinced that we cannot experience the fullness of what God has for us until the generations come together. We would not know about Joshua unless there was a Moses. We wouldn't see the double portion upon Elisha without Elijah. This has been God's heart from the beginning, and as we come closer to the last days we will see the generational gaps close as the church gets closer to the Father's heart.

I had just graduated from high school with hopes of going on to enjoy college life. I enrolled in a state college in West Virginia around the time my father launched a new church plant right across the river from the school. I found myself constantly going to the church, wanting to help Dad and getting involved with everything at the ministry. It was very evident within a few days that college was not for me, and I felt led to get a job and just serve at my father's new church. I don't think I knew what I was doing, but I knew I was being led.

Winters were terrible in West Virginia, and in the time between the beginning of the church service and the end, we could get two to three inches of snow. That's exactly what happened one particular Sunday morning. We were having service, and I noticed that snow was beginning to come down. All of a sudden there was so much snow I couldn't see out of the windows, and I knew we were in for a parking lot disaster. I remember going to the storage room and grabbing a snow shovel, broom, and salt. I knew it would be hard for some of the saints to get to their cars with snowy conditions like this. So I decided to shovel the sidewalk off, take a broom and knock the snow off the car windshields, and pour salt all over the place. It was just in my heart to serve.

While I was shoveling the last part of the sidewalk, tears began to flow down my cheeks, and I heard God's voice say clearly to me, "I have called you to preach!" I wasn't asking for it; I wasn't thinking about it; I was just doing my part to help the people of God get to their cars safely. Yet while I was "looking for donkeys," God began to show me my destiny!

This became a pattern for my life. Opportunities to serve became doors of destiny. Too many people think that because they are gifted and talented God is just going to open doors for them. The greatest in the kingdom are not the gifted or talented. Jesus said, "He who is greatest among you shall be your servant" (Matt. 23:11, MEV).

God is looking for those who will serve with or without recognition and do it as unto the Lord. Why should we serve? Because we love Jesus! This story about Saul at the beginning of this chapter illustrates a powerful truth that I believe we can all glean from because we need to learn that destiny is unlocked not when we seek our own will, but when we serve someone else's need.

You've probably heard stories about people who went to take care of someone else's need and in the process discovered their purpose. Someone started a homeless ministry because he came face-to-face with a homeless person. Someone went off to the mission field because she saw the face of an orphan on television or read about the problems in a remote village in Africa. Whatever God calls you to do, one thing is for certain: your destiny is locked up in the needs of the people around you. It's when you find and meet that need that a spark of destiny hits deep inside your spirit and something comes alive.

I will go a step further and say that it is usually while you are meeting the needs of others that you will connect with the people who will help unlock your destiny. If I had gone off to college, I wouldn't have served in my father's church. If I had not served in my father's church, I would not have met Dr. Lowery. If I had not served Dr. Lowery, I would have never met Perry Stone. If I had not met Perry Stone, I would not be the pastor of the Omega Center International in Cleveland, Tennessee, today.

It all started with serving my father's dream. Take a moment and look back over your life, and you will discover that while you were meeting someone else's need, God connected you to someone or something that has impacted your own life. It's just the way God works. You can't live as Jesus lived and have things not work for your good! To further discover the principle of serving the leader or mentor God puts in your life, let's take a look at the story of Saul chasing his father's donkeys of destiny.

Saul came from a very wealthy and powerful family. His father was Kish, whom the Bible called "a mighty man of wealth." The Bible says that Saul was a choice and handsome son who was head and shoulders taller than any of the people. He also was from the tribe of Benjamin, which is the smallest of all the tribes.

Kish had an issue that brought Saul on the scene of Bible history. His first assignment was not winning a battle or destroying false idols; it was finding his father's donkeys. For a wealthy family this seemed like an insignificant task. Why not go out and buy some new donkeys? But the issue we are dealing with here is not a matter of money but of stewardship.

Stewardship is a principle taught frequently throughout the Scriptures. Mankind was created in a garden and given dominion over every living thing. We were made stewards of God's creation; God put man in the Garden of Eden "to tend and keep it" (Gen. 2:15). Also, Jesus spoke very directly about the issue of stewardship in the parable of the talents. To the man who was a good steward Jesus said, "Well done, you good and faithful servant. You have been faithful over a few things. I will make you ruler over many things" (Matt. 25:23, MEV). But one of the verses I believe is essential in discussing this issue of stewardship is Luke 16:10, "He who is faithful in what is least is faithful also in much" (MEV).

I believe this is why God chose Joshua to succeed Moses as leader of the nation of Israel. He was faithful in little. If you want the Lord to promote you to a place of influence, it usually won't begin with a heroic adventure. The Lord will begin giving us opportunity to prove ourselves in what seem like insignificant ways. Before we look further into this story of Saul, let's take a brief detour to learn a lesson from Joshua.

JOSHUA WAS CARING FOR THE WEAK

Before Joshua became the great leader of the children of Israel, the one who brought them into the Promised Land, the Bible says "Joshua did what Moses had commanded and fought the army of Amalek" (Exod. 17:10, NLT). There are so many lessons we could learn from this one man's life, but I just want to point out this one quality in this chapter. What Joshua did is the best way to begin learning from the leader God places in authority in your life: do what is commanded from the leader you are serving.

God will always place a leader over you to help prepare you for your destiny. Sometimes that leader is great, and at times that leader can be extremely demanding, but either way the connection will help prepare you for where God is taking you. Some leaders show you what to do, and others will show you what not to do, but both the good and the bad are preparation for the plans God has for your life. Trust God with the leaders He places around you. Believe that He will use them to get you where He wants you to go.

Fortunately for Joshua, he was under Moses, a man considered one of the greatest leaders of all time. In Exodus 17 Moses had called the men of Israel to war with God's enemies, the Amalekites. While Moses, Aaron, and Hur were on the top of the mountain as God's authority, Joshua was in the valley carrying out the orders Moses gave. And because of this alignment of authority and obedience, the Bible declares in Exodus 17:13, "Joshua overwhelmed the army of Amalek in battle" (NLT).

In this generation we have a skewed idea of what it means to be a leader. You don't become a leader to get access to the mountaintop. God establishes you as a leader as you serve and meet people's needs. Too many just want to be on the mountaintop with Moses when they need to be in the valley fighting and serving the people. In church circles, many people think leadership is about getting in the green room with the special guests instead of helping to prepare the sanctuary for those attending the conference. If we really want to become great in God's kingdom, it starts with getting under the authority of God's leader in your life, being obedient to that person's commands, and faithfully serving others. When this happens in our churches, we will see what it looks like for generations to come together to live in victory.

Joshua's first order from Moses was to fight the army of Amalek. It is very significant that this was the first enemy Israel was commanded to war against. Deuteronomy 25:18 says this of the Amalekites: "How he met you on the way and attacked your rear ranks, all the stragglers at your rear, when you were tired and weary; and he did not fear God." The Amalekites attacked only the weak and the feeble in the back of the camp to plunder and take spoils. You may have been aware of that, but I want to give you some fresh perspective on this story.

In Exodus 17 Moses approached Joshua with the orders to lead an offensive strike against these Amalekites. To put this in more modern terms, Moses asked Joshua to risk his life to eliminate the enemy who was destroying those who seemed weak and insignificant. This is why Joshua's willingness to obey the orders to take care of the Amalekites is so powerful, because most people aren't willing to be faithful in the little things, especially when they see no value in it. Joshua was willing to fight the Amalekites, thus preventing them from attacking the weak and feeble of Israel.

I have met many young leaders who have great dreams and strong ambitions. These next-gen leaders can talk vision and share their overwhelming passion for their dream, but they aren't willing to take care of the little details because they seem insignificant to them. If the task doesn't give them recognition or benefit them in some way, they mark it as too insignificant to further their destiny. They would rather meet a person they believe can open a door for them than serve a person who really needs them. Jesus sees our hearts. Many do not become successful in the kingdom because if it's all about them now, when they barely have influence, how proud will they be when they do have great influence? God is not going to exalt someone who carries the same character trait that got Lucifer cast out of heaven.

Jesus taught His disciples about faithfulness. Everywhere Jesus went thousands would gather to be part of His ministry. Then one day in the midst of the crowds Jesus pulled His disciples to the side and shared with them the parable of the talents found in Matthew 25:14–30. His life lesson for them was that if they were faithful in the little things they would be trusted with much. Jesus knows our hearts and that we desire to do big things. But if in our pride we look to the big things and forget the reason we wanted to do those big things, why would God raise us up? Our purpose as leaders is to serve people, not to be served. If we will be faithful to serve in the little, we will be faithful to continue to serve in the bigger things.

This principle of serving and fighting for what we consider to be insignificant exposes a greater truth. When we are not willing to fight for the insignificant, we are proving that we don't carry the heart of Christ. Jesus didn't come to build Himself an empire, though He was gifted enough to do so. Jesus came to the least of these in order to serve them and manifest to them the incredible love of God. This is a lesson we all must learn. When God puts someone in a position of authority over you and that person gives you a task that seems simple, insignificant, and worthless, remember Joshua. He did not fight the Amalekites for popularity. By following Moses's leadership, Joshua was serving the weak and feeble around him.

When God sees you being faithful in the small things, He will trust you with more responsibility. As born-again believers we live in a kingdom that is upside down compared to the world's system. In the world, if you want to become great you have to be seen doing great things. But in the kingdom of God, if you want to become great you must be faithful to God's priorities when no one sees you. Greatness is found in what you do in secret.

How can you become like Joshua? Be faithful in the tasks you are given by the leaders God places over you. Don't allow the enemy to tell you the assignment is of no importance. If it weren't important, you wouldn't have been asked to do it. Remember that your faithfulness in the little things, especially the things others can't see, is what is qualifying you for greater kingdom responsibility. Do it in secret, and God will reward you in public!

IT'S ABOUT MORE THAN DONKEYS

Now back to Saul. He had been sent on an assignment to find his father's donkeys. What is so significant about finding these donkeys? These donkeys were part of his family's livelihood. These donkeys were part of his father's ability to provide for his children. Donkeys were used to carry tools and loads. They were also used to travel and get from one place to another. The donkeys were not that important to Saul because he didn't own them nor had he invested in them, but he cared for his father and was willing to serve him. This was the humble beginning of Israel's first king.

"Why go look for the donkeys? They are not your assignment." This is the response of a selfish generation.

Because the donkeys aren't ours and we have no vested interest in them, we don't think it necessary to go on a journey to find some dumb animals. We write it off as insignificant and not worthy of our time because it won't take us where we want to go. We want to find the right connections. But I have found that God's favor is more often seen on those who are serving than on the opportunists who are trying to climb the ladder of success without serving. God will exalt the humble and bring low the proud. This is a law of the kingdom. The greatest among us is the servant of all.

The assignment was so important to Saul that he went to the prophet for his father's sake and not his own. This is one of the last points I want to make about this story. If you are to serve faithfully, it starts by communicating with God not for your own benefit but for the benefit of others, especially the leader you've been called to serve. Saul found out that he was in the land where Samuel, the great prophet of Israel, was living. Saul knew that Samuel could tell him where these donkeys were. And while Saul was inquiring of God's man concerning his father's possession, he found his destiny. This brings me back to my initial point at the beginning of the chapter. When we are willing to serve an old man's dream, God opens up a young man's vision.

Saul wasn't chosen as king because he came from a wealthy family. He was not chosen as king because of his good looks or tall stature. Saul was chosen as king because he was willing to search for what seemed to most people to be insignificant. If you're in a position where you feel overlooked, don't forget that it is God who grants promotion and He never overlooks your acts of service. So the next time you are sent on a journey to look for some ole donkeys, remember that could be the moment God reveals destiny.

When we serve someone else's dream, we are opening doors for our God-ordained vision. How can that be? Jesus said, "And if you have not been faithful in that which is another man's, who will give you that which is your own?" (Luke 16:12, MEV). Don't complain about someone else's donkeys, because God will use them to lead you to your destiny!

What are you doing in this season of your life that seems insignificant in the eyes of man? Ask God to show you the value of the little things you are stewarding. When you do, you will begin to see by revelation of God's Spirit that those little things are the keys to opening the large doors of your God-ordained destiny. Don't murmur or complain. It just might be the day that an insignificant task turns into an unexplainable promotion.

Don't dodge requests to look for ole donkeys; they are the very thing that led to Saul being anointed the first king of Israel. I wish our current leaders would remember this principle. We have leaders today who don't fight for the weak and seemingly insignificant things. Maybe that's why millions of babies are aborted in the United States each year and so many orphans are neglected.

My prayer is that you will be like Joshua and Saul and fight for what seems insignificant. Leaders like that meet the needs of the people, and meeting their needs will open a door for us to be a godly influence in their lives. Let's change the world—and let's begin by serving the authorities God places in our lives, one act of simple obedience at a time.

A CONVERGENCE OF GENERATIONS

When talking with other leaders, whether in the church or in the marketplace, I notice a common thread in our conversations. At some point the discussion will turn to the different paradigms each generation has and the struggle to merge them together. There's a struggle between what the older generation has done and what the next generation wants to do. Oftentimes this can cause great frustration on both ends because we all do only what we have the revelation to do. However, I believe aspiring leaders must be careful to watch our attitudes, comments, and mind-sets, because we can quickly fall into the error of dishonor.

The truth is that God is doing a new thing. This is something people often say during generational transitions. Each generation carries a specific revelation that relates to the issues of their day. Moses's generation received the revelation of the Law. David's generation

received the revelation of the heart-to-heart relationship with God that goes beyond animal sacrifice. John
the Baptist's generation received the revelation of
repentance to see the kingdom of God in the earth.
Paul's generation received the revelation of the grace
of God in order to be transformed into the image of
Christ. If I were to continue on down the line, history
would prove this theory.

When the younger generation grows to maturity and
begins seeking the Lord, they receive revelation concerning what God wants to do in their day. In each generation God longs to build upon the ceiling the former
generation reached. God thinks generationally, and
this is clearly laid out in Scripture when He describes
Himself as the God of Abraham, Isaac, and Jacob. God
thinks long-term and sees the big picture. Where we
often miss what God is doing is when we see only our
part of the picture and not how it fits into God's grand
masterpiece. So instead of allowing different revelations to collide and create a beautiful mosaic in time,
we want to fight about whose piece God is going to use.
Let me let you in on a little secret: God is going to use
all the pieces! God is going to take what the former generation received and compound it with the fresh revelation God is giving to the new generation.

What we cannot afford to do in this hour is to build
monuments and sacred cows around our revelation of
what God is doing, because He is always on the move.
Some things are going to remain constant. God's Word
does not change. Hell is still a real place. The blood of
Jesus will never lose its power. The stripes upon Jesus's

back still provide healing to His children. These things will not change despite what some leaders in the church today will tell you.

However, even though doctrine does not change, sometimes God will put more emphasis on a specific doctrine in a particular generation. That doesn't make one generation totally right or totally wrong; it is just that God is saying something particular in that moment. But we are so quick to build monuments around the revelation that came during a certain era. Someone received a revelation about the blood of Jesus twenty years ago, and then someone else wrote a song about it, and then someone else wrote a best-selling book about it, and so we built monuments. Then when another generation comes along emphasizing something other than the blood of Jesus, we think what they're saying isn't of God. Get rid of the monuments and join the movement of God in this hour. God never told us to build monuments around the revelation of a particular era. He wants us to be obedient to what He is saying now. (By the way, this applies outside the church walls too.)

When we become preference driven and not presence driven, when our priority is having what we want and not what God wants, we enter into a dangerous place. With this attitude we cannot prepare the next generation to succeed us. We end up discouraging the ones we are called to encourage into their destiny. What I believe God wants to do in this hour is to "turn the hearts of the fathers to the children, and the hearts of the children to their fathers" (Mal. 4:6). In order for this to happen the church must begin to think generationally.

This will come with many challenges, but I want to focus on what we as young leaders must do when things go wrong with the authority God puts in our lives. How are we to respond when those over us are overlooking our calling, gifting, ability, or purpose? I believe that even as we see the previous generation's flaws, we need to look at the Word of God and determine in our hearts that we will honor those who have gone before us, because this is how we will see the convergence of generations and proper succession take place in the body of Christ.

Not everyone gets the privilege of having an Elijah or Moses leading them. Some people are placed under Saul, who was insecure in his leadership. No matter the person, situation, or circumstance, we must determine that we will not forfeit our inheritance through dishonor. That is why we must know what to do when things go wrong with the leader we are serving!

I Can't Fight With Your Armor

The transition from King Saul to King David is an incredible story about authority, leadership, and generational transition. It was a time of great victories for Israel, but at the same time the story reveals a deep inner struggle between the generations. To those on the outside I'm sure Israel looked prosperous, but inside his heart, King Saul was in chaos. What should have been a vibrant, synergistic relationship between the generations turned into a deadly battle because a king couldn't stand the fact that God decided to use someone else who happened to be a younger misfit of a man. Let's look at how Saul and David's relationship began.

In 1 Samuel chapter 17 we find Saul and his army encamped in the Valley of Elah, prepared for a battle with the Philistines. As the armies faced off on the mountainside, a loud shout would come from the back side of the Philistine camp as a giant named Goliath stepped into the Valley of Elah. Every morning and evening this giant would taunt Israel, challenging them to bring one man to fight against him. If the giant prevailed Israel would surrender, but if the giant lost Israel would be declared the victor. It seemed like an impossible task. Not only was the giant over nine feet tall, but his armor weighed hundreds of pounds. Not one person from Saul's army was willing to go against him, so there they sat, idle on the hillside.

Meanwhile, David, a ruddy, misfit teenager, was in the hills of Bethlehem tending to his father's sheep. David had brothers who were serving on the battlefield while he was left at the house taking care of his father's business. But then one day David's father, Jesse, called for him. Jesse had made a food basket for his boys and the captain of their troop, and he wanted David to take it to them and return with a report about his brothers' well-being.

So David got up early in the morning to carry out his father's orders. Upon arriving at Israel's camp, he greeted his brothers, and while they were talking there was an interruption. Goliath, the giant, began blaspheming God and the people of God. The Bible says

David heard every word Goliath said, and he saw that the men of Israel were afraid.

On that day, destiny came knocking upon the door of David's heart. This misfit, who spent his days worshipping and adoring God Almighty in the shepherd's fields, heard someone blaspheme his God! David's response was not to run in fear, but to say, "Who is this uncircumcised Philistine that he should defy the armies of the living God?" (1 Sam. 17:26, MEV).

When Eliab, David's oldest brother, heard David say this, he became angry with David. Eliab mistook David's passion for God as pride and insolence of heart. Because of David's relationship with God, he had a perspective the others who were working for God did not have. This perspective can come only from someone who has been with God in secret and knows His Word.

David's response to his brother was, "Is there not a cause?" (1 Sam. 17:29). Another way of saying this is, "Is there not a word from God?" According to the Law of Moses, which David would have known, this uncircumcised Philistine who blasphemed God was to be stoned.

David's passionate response to Goliath got back to King Saul, so the king called for him. David's first words to the king were, "Let no man's heart fail because of him [Goliath]; your servant will go and fight with this Philistine" (1 Sam. 17:32). Saul, out of concern for the young man who had only a slingshot and a stone, offered David his armor. So David tried on Saul's armor, which included a bronze helmet and a coat of mail.

David fastened his sword to the armor, but he could not walk. The armor did not fit.

David was not able to wear the pieces of Saul's armor because he had not tested them. They didn't fit him, and they were not the tools God had used to train David in the wilderness. He knew how to sling rocks as a shepherd, not how to fight like a soldier in the military.

The principle we need to learn from this part of the story is that Saul and David were on the same side—the Lord's side. Goliath was the enemy of God and Israel, and Saul and David had the same mission: to kill Goliath so Israel could prevail. But this is where we sometimes get messed up in the generational transfer. Don't get mad at David for not wearing Saul's armor. David is out to fulfill the same mission Saul has, but David must do it the way the Lord trained him to as a shepherd.

Let me get more practical and share a personal story. A couple of years ago I went to preach at a church in Kentucky. During these services, I noticed that the church was full of young people, and there were hardly any adults present for the service. I thought that maybe because I was so young the church assumed the service was for youth. But then I noticed that the church had very modern lighting and technology, so I began to think it was geared toward youth alone. However, when I asked the pastor about the situation, his response revealed why the adults were not coming.

Just a year prior to my visit to this church, the older generation began praying for their sons and daughters to get saved. So the pastor said, "Let's start implementing new worship and technology in the church to attract the younger generation to the services. The people were praying, the church was remodeling, and transition began to take place in the church. The sons and daughters were beginning to get saved, and they wanted to get involved. So new worship teams were created along with dance and drama teams, and new outreaches were developed to reach the lost. God was answering the prayers of the older generation right before their eyes.

But by the time I arrived, the adults were missing. Why? The sad reason is that the older people didn't like the change. They didn't like the new songs, new technology, and new methods of ministry. The older members were angry because "David" wasn't willing to wear "Saul's" armor. They'd prayed for change, and now that God was answering their prayers, they were more concerned with methods than seeing the mission fulfilled.

We all know how the David and Goliath story ends. David triumphs over the giant with a sling and a stone. It is a powerful story that shows that it takes a love relationship with God to slay giants. All the men who had been trained for war were not willing to face this giant. But one passionate God seeker took a rock and slew the enemy that all Israel feared. And this victory placed David in Saul's house to serve as his armor bearer.

CALLED TO SERVE

The Bible says that Saul took David that day and would not let him go home to his father again. Saul was going to take this giant killer and make a mighty man out of him. Saul was very proud to have this brave young man as a part of his kingdom, and David's victory caused Israel to rejoice for the great things the Lord was doing. I think there is nothing more powerful than seeing the generations work together. So David became Saul's armor bearer and was set over the men of war (1 Sam. 18:5). The Bible says that David behaved wisely and was accepted in the sight of all the people, including Saul's servants. In other words, he had incredible favor upon his life.

Many of you reading this book are going to experience this in your own life. When you do something incredible that captures the attention of those around you, someone will want to bring you under his care in order to make you great. When that happens, take the time to allow him to make that investment. You may be young, passionate, and bursting with vision, but you need wisdom. Why go through the school of hard knocks when you can serve under someone who can teach you their successes and failures and keep you from pitfalls that could cost you dearly?

In order for the generations to truly work together, emerging leaders must be found faithful in service and honor those who have gone before. Even though David had been anointed king (1 Sam. 16:13) and his victory over Goliath was a huge success for the nation, that didn't automatically make him king. During this season he was called to serve under Saul. Many times in the church and in the business world, younger workers think they are ready to start their own thing the first time they experience success. One miracle of healing doesn't qualifying you to start a ministry of your own. One great idea doesn't mean you should go out and start your own business. You need to find someone to serve and sit under until you have been processed for the purpose God has for you.

As I mentioned, David became Saul's armor bearer. When I first began working for Dr. Lowery, one the very first books that was placed into my hand was *God's Armor Bearer* by Terry Nance. I learned so many lessons from this book. It truly helped me understand what it means to lay down one's life for another. The Hebrew word for *armor bearer* paints a picture of someone who lifts up his leader to assist him and protect him against the enemies that come to destroy him.

Terry Nance writes in *God's Armor Bearer* that an armor bearer is to provide strength to the leader while having deep respect for that leader and tolerance of his personality and way of doing things.[1] One of the harder concepts he shares is that we must possess endless strength so as to press that leader onward without giving way under harsh treatment.

Let's face it. Even though God has called believers to work together generationally, there will be differences. The fact that God calls us to serve under someone doesn't mean we will like everything about the person we are working with. It does, however, mean that we must humble ourselves, choose the way of love according to 1 Corinthians 13, and be determined to not get offended. The opportunity to get offended will always be there, but we can guard against it by avoiding pride, because pride is the seed of offense.

When serving under an older leader, we must be like David and behave wisely (1 Sam. 18:5). There are generational differences not only in revelation but also in mentalities and personalities. We must be willing to submit to another generation's ideas and respectfully offer ours. If the leader doesn't accept your idea, don't get offended. Just pray for that person's heart to be open to your voice, and expect God to move in the situation.

You must remember that God knows what you are capable of, and He knows that you have the ability to do amazing things. He is the One who created you, and He knows exactly where you are in your journey to your dream. He knows the person you are serving under! It's all on purpose.

When God-Given Authority Throws Spears

David had just returned home from slaughtering a Philistine giant, and the women came out of all the cities to meet King Saul. The music was playing, and everyone was rejoicing. That's when the daughters of Israel began to sing, "Saul has slain his thousands, and David his ten thousands" (1 Sam. 18:7). This is where the story gets very interesting. In 1 Samuel 18:8 the Bible says, "Saul became very angry, and this saying was displeasing to him. Therefore he said, 'They have ascribed to David ten thousands, but to me they have ascribed thousands. Now what remains for him to have but the kingdom?'" (MEV). In that moment pride opened the gate, and jealousy filled Saul's heart.

The very next day a distressing spirit came upon Saul. In order to serve Saul, David came to Saul playing his harp to soothe the king's weariness. But while David was playing his harp and serving the king, Saul threw a spear at David intended to pin him to the wall. Here is David, willing to give everything to his leader, and now spears are being thrust toward his body. Can you imagine what was going through David's mind?

The issue was this: Saul's pride caused him to misinterpret the rejoicing of the people. The daughters of Israel were singing about the synergy of Saul and David, but jealousy caused him to hear the women comparing their numbers. They were singing "Saul has slain his thousands, and David his ten thousands." But Saul heard, "Saul has slain his thousands, *but* David his ten thousands." Pride will always cause you to interpret the praise of someone else as competition instead of hearing it for what it truly is.

We must learn to harness the power of synergy. The Scripture declares that one can put a thousand to flight, but two can put ten thousand. (See Deuteronomy 32:30 and Romans 4:20.) It was God's will for Saul and David to work together and destroy Israel's enemies, but because of his pride, Saul was ready to slay the man who was helping him accomplish ten times more than he could do by himself. This is sad, but it's happening in churches all across America. God is sending the

Davids of this generation to ministries, and when the sons and daughters become successful, the older leaders don't see synergy, they feel competition. The day Saul became jealous and tried to kill David, the Bible says, "Saul was suspicious of David from that day and forward" (1 Sam. 18:9, MEV).

Instead of Saul embracing the power of the generations working together, he became suspicious of David. Remember, they were working together to slay ten thousands in battle, yet Saul was only concerned about people's opinions when he was back at home. I have told people this for years: when it comes to teamwork, I would rather be a productive nobody on a team that wins championships than a superstar on a team that loses every game.

We need to recognize what God is doing right now; He is bringing convergence of generations to slay ten thousands of our enemies. It is to be a time of acceleration in seeing the kingdom of darkness destroyed and the kingdom of God established. This will happen only when we get out of our personality-driven concepts and into generational synergy.

We need a revelation about two rivers right here in the United States of America. The mighty Mississippi River is known all over the world, but what really makes the Mississippi mighty? It becomes mighty because of the synergy of the Ohio River. The Ohio River is not as powerful as the Mississippi, but without its strength the Mississippi would not be as grand.

The Ohio River represents the older generation that has been a consistent force, and the Mississippi represents this new generation. We need to see this in the spirit, because God wants the older generation to supply the support, power, and encouragement to make the next generation a mighty force that the enemy cannot contain. It's time for synergy to come to the generations!

OH, HOW THE MIGHTY HAVE FALLEN

For years this jealous leader, Saul, tried his best to end David's life. David spent many years living in the caves of the Judean wilderness all because someone in leadership over him could only see him as competition. David didn't feel the same way; he had more than one opportunity to take Saul's life, but time after time David said he would not touch God's anointed.

You might be wondering how David could call Saul God's anointed, since David had been anointed king and Saul was busy trying to kill him. It is because at one time that was true. God chose Saul to be king over Israel, and for a season Saul allowed himself to be used by God to do mighty things for the Lord. Because David knew the Lord's heart, he kept a proper perspective of Saul as God's chosen despite the way he was being treated.

In his book *A Tale of Three Kings*, Gene Edwards shares a powerful truth concerning why God allowed this terrible leader to persecute David. Saul's purpose in David's life was to get the Saul out of David. God will at times allow you to sit under illegitimate authority to make sure all that is illegitimate is removed out of you so you won't make the same mistakes when you assume a position of authority. Now, Saul and David had some good days together, and those are the ones you should hold tight to your chest if you are currently serving under a Saul today. But in the end, when David learned Saul's fate, David became a powerful example to young or emerging leaders.

David's response to Saul's death was not, "Oh, thank God!" Nor was it, "It's about time." Even though David was thoroughly qualified to say those things in the natural, David decided to operate in a kingdom concept called honor! David responded to Saul's death by saying, "How the mighty have fallen in the midst of battle!" (2 Sam. 1:25).

How could David call the man who tried to kill him mighty? How could he honor the man who drove him out of his house with spears and chased him into a cave? David was able to do that because he knew that the way he responded to the king would one day affect the way he would lead. The thing I truly love about David is that, no matter what, David wanted to do what was right in the sight of the Lord. That's what I want for your life. Even if you are under a leader who is threatened by you, just remember what the Bible says of David: that he behaved wisely. And because of that, God was with him.

There will come a day when you will leave that church or that job. Whether you are forced out or called out, you will have a decision to make. Will you pass the test when authority goes wrong? When you leave will you honor that leader or try to kill his reputation?

David has one more lesson to teach us about exiting from a terrible leader. Saul had perished, and the young man who ended Saul's life came bragging to David about how the king was dead. The young man thought David would be pleased, but instead David tore his clothes and said, "How is it that you did not fear raising your hand to destroy the anointed of the Lord?" (2 Sam. 1:14, MEV). Then David had the young man executed.

Why did David react so harshly to this young man? It is because this young man did not choose the path of the kingdom, which is honor. The law and the prophets hinge upon this principle, "Therefore, everything you would like men to do to you, do also to them" (Matt. 7:12, MEV). David knew one day he would lead the great nation of Israel, and how he responded in this season would determine how the next generation would treat him!

So, I have one last question for you. How do you want to be treated when it's your season to lead? With honor? Then begin learning to operate in honor no matter what you have to go through. Stay fully submitted to authority. Don't allow the enemy to make you a Saul by throwing spears back at the person misusing his or her authority. Instead, humbly submit to God's Word and know that one day He will raise you up to be a blessing to those you are called to lead. I choose honor, because I want to see synergy between my generation and the next!

Let it be said of the generations leading the church today that instead of throwing spears, we walked in synergy. We chose to accept the different revelations and mentalities of each generation and worked together to slay the giants of our day. We need to decide today what kind of victory we want to see later. We can choose not to submit to one another and slay our thousands, or we can walk in synergy to slay our ten thousands. The choice is ours, and if we are faithful to walk in unity, the world will be drawn to the light of Jesus Christ's glorious gospel.

CHAPTER II

GIVING IS WORTH MORE IN SECRET

W e are living in a moment in history when we as believers have an opportunity unlike in any other generation to shine in the midst of darkness. In order to do this, we will need a remnant of people who will refuse the popular, lukewarm church culture and embrace the "do it in secret" lifestyle that brings misfits into kingship. We can't afford to build our walk with God on passing fads; we must build our lives upon the rock-solid truths of Jesus's Word.

Many Americans have experienced the effect of a declining economy in the United States. Perhaps you are one of them. If you haven't experienced a job loss or economic hardship since 2008, you probably know someone who has. But economic ups and downs don't have to dictate the level of our prosperity. God has promised that those who are faithful to sow in secret will be rewarded publicly. This happens when we under-stand the power of giving.

We have the opportunity to demonstrate the power of the kingdom by giving the way Jesus commanded us to. The lifestyle that brings misfits into kingship is about living in an intimate relationship with the Father that unlocks our God-ordained destiny. This, in turn, causes His glory to be seen in this world.

I believe God is about to do some things in our day that people will know only God could have made happen. This is why it is so critical for us to live a secret life with God, because sometimes we can try and take credit for what God is doing. But the Bible says God will not share His glory with another (Isa. 42:8; 48:11). This is a truth that I am praying everyone reading this book will grasp. We are stepping into a time when God is going to fill the earth with His glory, and we can't afford to try to take credit for it.

If you want to look at the life of someone who was concerned about getting all the glory, look no further than King Saul. As we saw in the previous chapter, he couldn't stand that one of his young leaders was being celebrated for slaying a giant. So envy filled his heart and opened a door for him to be tormented by evil spirits. Saul did what he thought was right instead of what God said to do, and rather than repent of his actions he built a memorial to himself (1 Sam. 15).

The day that Saul got in the way of God's glory is the day God chose another king. Please hear me. In your pursuit of changing the world, stay humble and learn to listen to the voice of God. When He speaks, do all that He has told you to do. Then when men see the marvelous things God has done through your life, give Him all the glory, because the day you begin to build monuments for yourself is the day God may give your assignment to someone else.

This is why it is so important to understand the principle of giving. One of the things that I believe will keep us from taking God's glory is developing a giving heart. One of the first sermons Jesus ever preached concerning the "do it in secret" life is found in Matthew 6. The Scripture says:

> Be sure that you not do your charitable deeds before men to be seen by them. Otherwise you have no reward from your Father who is in heaven. Therefore, when you do your charitable deeds, do not sound a trumpet before you as the hypocrites do in the synagogues and in the streets, that they may be honored by men. Truly I say to you, they have their reward. But when you do your charitable deeds, do not let your left hand know what your right hand is doing, that your charitable deeds may be in secret. And your Father who sees in secret will Himself reward you openly.
>
> —MATTHEW 6:1–4, MEV

Notice that Jesus dealt again with the mind-set of a hypocrite. He said hypocrites want people to see them as extravagant givers so they can receive the glory of men. In this passage Jesus is exposing the fact that we should never live for the praise of men but to honor and obey God. The applause of men goes only so far.

As I prayed about writing this chapter, I asked the Lord why He wanted to teach a generation how to "do it in secret." I immediately sensed the Holy Spirit say, "Because I don't want them to settle for the glory of men when they were destined to walk in the glory of God." My heart yearns for everyone to grasp this truth. We have settled for men's applause and worldly success, but those things come and go. God's approval, acceptance, favor, and glory are for all eternity.

God doesn't want us to base our success in life upon the unstable, hard-hearted opinions of men. Since the fall of man, we have been an unreliable source of love. That's why God wants us to live for His glory and not the praise of men. Peter the Apostle reminds us that "all flesh is as grass, and all the glory of man as the flower of grass. The grass withers, and its flower falls away" (1 Pet. 1:24, MEV). In other words, don't settle for living for the temporal praise of men when you can live for the eternal glory of God.

When you spend time in the secret place, you will find that God not only rewards your private obedience in this life, but those times will sustain you for all eternity. Those God moments that begin in the unseen soil of your heart manifest in public. Once you have experienced the glory of God because of your private obedience, you will never settle for the glory of men. You will burn to live in the glory of God.

Delivered From the Yeast
of the Pharisees

We must be careful not to enter into the subtle sins of the Pharisees. Jesus warned His disciples in Luke 12:1, saying, "Beware of the yeast of the Pharisees, which is hypocrisy" (MEV). Giving to the poor and to the work of God is a great Christian duty, but our hearts must be pure and our motivation must be to please God. The goal of giving is to be obedient to God, not to draw attention to ourselves.

Giving is not something Jesus considered optional but rather something expected of us as followers of Christ. In Matthew 6:1–4, Jesus is talking about the "giving of alms," or giving to the poor. In that day the Jews had a box called "the box of righteousness," which was dedicated to helping the poor. When one is obedient to this command, Christ promises great reward, but the great reward is lost if the giving is done hypocritically.

The religious of that day fulfilled their obligation to give in the "box of righteousness," but their motivation was neither obedience to God nor the love of people. They were simply doing it to show how "holy" they were. Their motivation was pride, and their goal was to boast. This is why Jesus called them hypocrites. The Greek word is *hypokrites*, which means an actor or stage player. In that day, an actor could play several parts by wearing different masks.

These religious leaders were just playing a part to make a good show. When they wanted to be religious, they would pull out the religious mask. But Jesus said behind the mask these men were "whitewashed tombs, which look beautiful on the outside but on the inside are full of the bones of the dead" (Matt. 23:27, NIV). These men gave to the poor only at the synagogue and in the streets, where the greatest number of people could see them. This is the reason Jesus said we must not be like the hypocrites—because their motivation is wrong.

Did these hypocrites receive a reward? After all, they were obedient to give to the poor. The answer is yes, they received a reward, but it was the temporal reward of man's applause. It was not the reward that God promises to give those who are obedient. Their motivation was for men to see them, so their reward was that men saw them. In other words, when you give a gift to be seen by man you block God from sending the gift He desires you to have. But when you learn to "do it in secret," you will never lose the promises God made to you.

Not only is the hypocrites' reward an earthly one, but their hypocrisy blocks their future reward in eternity. Jesus said those who give in obedience to God "shall be repaid at the resurrection of the just" (Luke 14:14, MEV). Do you want your reward now from men, or do you want to store up eternal rewards from God in the future? This is the reality of what Jesus is saying to His disciples. Don't sell yourself short of the blessings of God just to get a few pats on the back. Live for more!

GIVING: AN ISSUE OF THE HEART

Many people overlook the command to give because giving has been so abused over the years. But we cannot allow one generation's abuse to keep us from the blessing of obeying Christ. Giving is an essential part of the "do it in secret" lifestyle. I don't want to see another generation of believers come along who look good on the outside but whose hearts are not right. My prayer is that we do it right in this generation.

Giving is an issue of the heart. Jesus said, "For where your treasure is, there will your heart be also" (Matt. 6:21, MEV). There is a connection between our walk with God and how we steward our finances. Jesus talked about finances more than He spoke of heaven and hell combined. Even John the Baptist, the forerunner of Jesus, talked about finances when preaching about preparing the people for the kingdom (Luke 3:11–14).

Jesus also knows that money and possessions can so easily become idols in our lives. That's why He went on to say, "No one can serve two masters; for either he will hate the one and love the other, or else he will be loyal to the one and despise the other. You cannot serve God and mammon" (Matt. 6:24). One of the saddest stories in all of the Gospels is about the rich young ruler. This man had everything money could buy, but he couldn't give up his earthly possessions in order to gain a greater treasure (Matt. 19:21). Think of what this rich man gave up. He had an opportunity to follow Jesus—to see the miracles, to see with his eyes the dead being raised and the multitudes being fed with five loaves of bread and two fish. Yet he missed the opportunity to know the very Son of God all because his heart was worshipping another god—mammon.

It was this man's possessions that kept him from participating in the greatest moment of history. What a foolish decision, because when this man went to the grave he couldn't take his possessions with him. Jim Elliot, the missionary martyr, said, "He is no fool who gives what he cannot keep to gain what he cannot lose."[1]

Being a giver will protect you from worshipping the god of mammon and keep you pure toward God. For generations believers have sold out to this world to gain what they cannot keep as they lose the only thing that will last for eternity—being fully pleasing to God. What is the lesson to be learned here? Jesus is trying to teach us that there is more to live for.

He said: "Do not lay up for yourselves treasures on earth, where moth and rust destroy and where thieves break in and steal; but lay up for yourselves treasures in heaven, where neither moth nor rust destroys and where thieves do not break in and steal. For where your treasure is, there your heart will be also" (Matt. 6:19–21).

YOUR MONTH OF FINANCIAL BREAKTHROUGH

I had been working for the T. L. Lowery Global Ministries for nearly four years when God spoke to me that it was time to launch out into my personal ministry. This did not happen quickly, but through a series of events, and several prophetic words and confirmation, I began the process of transition. It wasn't an easy thing to do in the natural because so many things were at stake.

I had just recently purchased my first house; we'd just had our first son, and then found out three months later that we were pregnant with the second. I had a good job with consistent pay plus a vehicle that Dr. Lowery allowed me to drive. My life was in a very comfortable place. But I have learned over the years that God will allow you to be comfortable for a season, then He will put your hands to the plow for a kingdom assignment.

I remember asking God how I was going to launch out into my own ministry and be able to sustain my family. How would I pay my bills, keep gas in the car, and buy groceries for my family? There was no guarantee of any appointments or finances. God's response was Proverbs 24:11: "Rescue those being led away to death; hold back those staggering toward slaughter" (NIV). I appreciated the direction God was giving to me. I had the "why" answered, but now what I felt I needed was the "how."

Finally, after three days of prayer, God gave me the "how" when He spoke these words into my spirit one morning: *"I don't want you to send out letters, make phone calls, or create a website. I want you to find a secret place to pray and read My Word. While you are spending time with Me, I will put your name in pastors' spirits, and they will invite you to come preach."* This was God's strategic plan for launching the ministry He had entrusted to me.

I still remember driving away from the T. L. Lowery Global Ministry Center with great expectancy in my spirit while in my flesh I was thinking to myself, "You are losing your mind." I had no guaranteed income and no appointments or promises to preach anywhere. It was just God and me and what He had said to me.

I asked a minister friend of mine if I could use an extra office he had as my secret place to pursue God each day. So there I'd go day after day, seeking God. Almost a week into seeking God's face, I thought to myself, "God, I don't know what You are doing, but I need some sign of hope." Then God reminded me of Matthew 6:33, "But seek first the kingdom of God and His righteousness, and all these things shall be added to you." So I set my face like flint to know God's will and make that my priority in prayer. I prayed for awakening, salvation, revival, healing, and for the nation to turn back to God. I forgot about getting appointments to preach and started focusing on His will. The very next week four different pastors called my phone to set up appointments.

Every pastor who called would say the same thing: "Mark, this week when I was praying for the church God kept speaking to me that you needed to come and minister to our people." Within a few weeks my schedule was full for nearly half the year. I had decided to quit focusing on my agenda and yield myself to His agenda. Matthew 6:33 was no longer a good scripture to quote; I had seen it manifest in my life. God was moving, and I was doing nothing but making His will my heart's desire.

Even though my schedule was full, the offerings honestly were not that great. I even went to one church where the pastor told the people, "Let's bless Brother Mark and his family. Let's get him a tank of gas and enough for a hamburger." That's exactly what they gave me. I filled my car up with gas and stopped by McDonald's with enough money to buy a cheeseburger. That's when I was hit with my first financial worry. I had no idea what I was going to do to pay our bills.

I went back to my secret place and asked God how I was going to pay the bills that month. His response: "This month will be your month for financial breakthrough." I came out of that time of prayer with my faith lifted and ready to take on the world. Two weeks went by and nothing happened. I had only four more days until my house payment and utilities were due. Then another day passed, and I was only two days away from being late on my house payment.

I don't want to leave out the part where I went to my PO Box every day, laid my hand in it, and prophesied that money was going to fill that box. I was speaking faith and proving my faith by going every day to the post office. But at this point I was just waiting. Two days before my bills were due I went to the mailbox and found two envelopes. You can imagine how I reacted to seeing those envelopes, especially when I realized they were not bills. Let's just say I had a little more pep in my step. I didn't wait to get in the car. I ripped those envelopes open, and there was a check in each one that was just enough to pay all of my bills.

But still I thought to myself, "God said this would be my month of financial breakthrough." Anyone who heard a word like that would think it meant an "above and beyond" type of blessing was on its way. Those two checks covered only what I needed to pay my bills. So after rejoicing for a brief moment, I wondered why there wasn't more. I knew what God had said and that He is the God of more than enough. So I began talking with God in the car and said, "God, You said this would be my month of financial blessing." I waited and then came the response: "It is your month of financial break-through, because now you have the faith to believe I can meet your every need."

When I felt that word in my spirit, an impartation of faith came into me. From that day to this one, I have never worried about my finances, where appointments would come from, or how God was going to move. I knew that no matter the situation, God would supply all of my needs according to His riches in glory.

When you devote your life to making His kingdom your agenda, it's no longer up to you to provide for yourself. God will begin to open the windows of heaven over your life and meet every need and remove every obstacle that stands in your path. I always say, "If you are in God's will then it's God's bill." Keep moving forward and watch Him supply. It's like the psalmist said, "I have been young, and now am old; yet I have not seen the righteous forsaken, nor their offspring begging bread" (Ps. 37:25, MEV).

STOP PRAYING THAT

My family and I were traveling all over the country as I preached revivals and church services. At the time we had just a little white Chevrolet Cobalt. Each time we left town, we had to fill the trunk with my wife's luggage and the kids' strollers, and everything else had to fit in the back. Every time we left home for another church, it looked like we were moving. We were crammed into that little car.

Just like every man of faith, I started complaining about traveling in that little car. I started praying that God would give us another vehicle, something bigger and more comfortable. After all, I was doing the will of God and knew it would be a blessing to my family. So day after day I found myself constantly thinking about needing a bigger vehicle. Then one day as I was praying about the vehicle, God interrupted my prayer and said, "Mark, stop praying for a vehicle and seek My kingdom. Isn't that how I proved Myself to you before?"

Talk about conviction! I was humbled by this state-ment and realized I had wasted precious time with God praying for material things instead of the things that really mattered. I immediately returned to praying pas-sionately for souls to be saved, the sick to be healed, and prison doors to open for the bound. I was consumed with a passion to see God's kingdom released upon the earth. For almost two months I prayed, and the vehicle never once crossed my mind. If God wanted me to have it, it would come as I sought His kingdom first.

Two months passed and I was invited to preach at a camp meeting in Hixson, Tennessee. I poured my heart and soul into that service, and little did I know that while I was doing God's will, God was speaking to another minister on the front row about my needs. God moved powerfully in the service, and I knew the will of God had been done. Nothing seemed to happen for me, but I was satisfied just knowing that God was using me to bless His people.

A few days later my phone rang. I didn't notice the number, but I answered anyway. When I heard the man's voice, I remembered him from the recent camp meeting. This particular minister asked me if I would be willing to come speak at an upcoming conference at his church. I was excited to even be considered to be a part of such a great event. But then the minister went on to say, "But Mark, I am only going to fly you in one way." To be honest it scared me because we didn't have a lot of money and I knew I couldn't afford a plane ticket back.

So I finished the conversation by saying that I would love to be a part of the conference, and I was just going to trust God with all the details. But before I got off the phone I had to ask him why he was flying me only one way. That's when he said, "Mark, I'm only flying you in one way because you are going to drive back in your new car." I almost dropped the phone. Within ten minutes he sent me an e-mail with all the specs on the vehicle. In the e-mail he explained that he was going to give us another vehicle, but the Lord spoke to him to give me the bigger one. I just laughed because he could have given me another little car, but God got involved in the details and today I still drive a large Nissan Armada.

The greatest thing God has ever done for me was rebuke me in the middle of praying for material things. It's this simple: God is not concerned with temporal things. He wants people to be concerned about fulfilling His will and being faithful to seek Him in secret. In this chapter I didn't get into being faithful in tithing, supporting world missions, and blessing people as the Spirit of God prompts us. That's because it was what happened in the secret place, the things no one knew about, that unlocked the public reward of a Nissan Armada that allowed me to more comfortably travel for ministry.

God's Word is true: "But my God shall supply your every need according to His riches in glory by Christ Jesus" (Phil. 4:19, MEV).

GIVING IN SECRET

Jesus said, "But when you do your charitable deeds, do not let your left hand know what your right hand is doing, that your charitable deeds may be in secret. And your Father who sees in secret will Himself reward you openly" (Matt. 6:3–4, MEV). From a rabbinical understanding of the text, the giving of the right hand is a sign of readiness and determination to be one who gives. This means that our hearts should be in such a place that when God prompts us to give and meet a need, we respond to His invitation with joyful obedience.

But we have a responsibility to keep it private. Our left hand should not know what our right hand is doing. In other words, we are not supposed to take delight in the fact that we have met a need. We are supposed to be His representation in the earth. We are supposed to follow His orders to be His hands and feet in the earth. It's not us meeting the need; it's Him touching lives through us.

You must understand that when you learn how to give in secret, you will begin to experience the way your Father rewards His children. The promise of Matthew 6:1–4 is that "your Father who sees in secret will Himself reward you openly" (Matt. 6:4, MEV). So what does God do for those who are faithful in the tithe, faithful in meeting needs, and faithful to help the least of these? Yes, they will store up treasures in heaven that no one or thing can steal from them, but there are benefits they can lay claim to on the earth as well.

When God spoke to Abram in Genesis 15:1, God described Himself as his "shield" and "exceedingly great reward." How does God reward? In the Sermon on the Mount, Jesus promises treasures that will be laid up for us in heaven. According to Psalm 112:5–9, as believers we will be secure in this life and the life to come; we will not be afraid of bad news, and our hearts will be firm. God will remember givers forever, our righteousness will endure forever, and we will triumph over our enemies.

Second Corinthians 9:6–11 tells us that God will make all grace abound toward us, that we will be able to have sufficiency in all things, and that we will have abundance for every good work. This passage stands in agreement with how God blessed Abraham. God told this great man of faith, "[In] blessing I will bless you" (Gen. 22:17). This shows that God rewards those who bless others by blessing them more so the cycle can continue. That's why 2 Corinthians 9:10 says, "Now He who supplies seed to the sower and supplies bread for your food will also multiply your seed sown and increase the fruits of your righteousness" (MEV).

When God finds a giver, He rewards him by multiplying what he has sown so he can continue to be a blessing. Scripture says, "There is one who scatters, yet increases; and there is one who withholds more than is right, but it leads to poverty" (Prov. 11:24, MEV). This is the power of giving in secret—God will make a way for you to continue doing it in secret.

Once you have found the fulfillment of meeting people's needs, you will sense God's approval, and people will see the blessing and promotion of a misfit right in front of their eyes. People will wonder how a misfit can get to where you are, so you will need to be ready to share your secret so the Rewarder can supply their every need.

CHAPTER 12

FAST-FORWARD

Many of us look for shortcuts to arrive at our destination faster. We are always in a hurry to get something done so we can move on to something else. It's a never-ending cycle. But there is a key to acceleration that most believers have forsaken. The lack of this discipline has caused entire nations to be shaken and leaders to be replaced. The key I am speaking of is the power of fasting.

You can search high and low in the volumes of history and you will not find a man or woman God used mightily who didn't practice the biblical discipline of fasting. This commitment to fasting is another aspect of the "do it in secret" lifestyle that turns misfits into kings. Jesus assumed those who followed Him would do this along with praying and giving.

Jesus said:

> Moreover, when you fast, do not be like the hypo-
> crites, with a sad countenance. For they disfigure
> their faces that they may appear to men to be
> fasting. Assuredly, I say to you, they have their
> reward. But you, when you fast, anoint your head
> and wash your face, so that you do not appear
> to men to be fasting, but to your Father who is
> in the secret place; and your Father who sees in
> secret will reward you openly.
>
> —MATTHEW 6:16–18

In this passage Jesus again combats the pride that causes people to perform Christian duties for the praise of men instead of for the heavenly Father. We have already discussed why hypocrites pursue public affirmation—because they are more concerned about man's opinion than God's and ultimately forfeit their eternal reward before God.

If you want to experience true spiritual growth and clear direction for your destiny, fasting is not optional, but necessary. There is a movement in the church today that says that because of grace we are not obligated to fast anymore. It claims we have been liberated from the disciplines of self-denial, even though this does not line up with Scripture. In Matthew 6, Jesus said, "When you fast . . ." That wasn't just for the disciples when He walked the earth, but for all who choose to follow Him.

When John's disciples asked the Son of God why His disciples did not fast, Jesus said, "Can the friends of the bridegroom mourn as long as the bridegroom is with them? But the days will come when the bridegroom will be taken away from them, and then they will fast" (Matt. 9:15). Jesus was telling them that after His resurrection the disciples would fast. What would the purpose of their fast be? To keep their hearts tender and yearning for the day when their fellowship with Jesus would not be by spirit only, but face-to-face.

Fasting, or abstaining from food or whatever God calls you to sacrifice, is a powerful weapon at the believer's disposal. Ezra led one of the first trips back to Israel after God's people had spent seventy years in Babylonian captivity. They had a long journey back home and knew they would walk through land occupied by their enemies. But they didn't ask the king for soldiers to escort them. Instead, Ezra called the people to a fast. That moved the hand of God, and He led Ezra and the people back to Israel safely (Ezra 8:21–23).

In 2 Chronicles 20:2–4 King Jehoshaphat was told that a vast army was coming against Judah. The king did not begin assembling the troops or taking inventory of their weapons. Instead he called all of Judah to a fast and inquired of the Lord. Their fast moved the hand of God, and Judah was preserved!

Those are just two examples from the Old Testament concerning the fruit of fasting. Besides protection, fasting unleashes power upon your life. That's why I want to spend this chapter exploring this lost discipline. Those who will hear the call to fasting and do it in secret will fast-forward their misfit-to-kingship process. I have found in my own life that with every fast, God seems to accelerate what He is doing in my life. I believe when you accept the call of fasting, you will find the same to be true for you.

THE PURPOSE OF FASTING

We live at a time when there are more self-led than Spirit-led believers because too many hearts have yet to be humbled. I believe the primary purpose of fasting is for us to humble ourselves under God's hand. Jesus told us who would be the greatest in the kingdom and whom God would exalt. He said, "Therefore whoever humbles himself like this child is the greatest in the kingdom of heaven" (Matt. 18:4, MEV). Christ continued this thought when He said, "For those who exalt themselves will be humbled, and those who humble themselves will be exalted" (Matt. 23:12, NIV).

In the religious culture of Jesus's day, the term *humble* was directly connected to the practice of fasting. King David said, "I humbled my soul with fasting" (Ps. 35:13, NAS). Fasting humbles your heart so the Lord can begin to move in your life and circumstances. The promises continue, "Humble yourselves before the Lord, and he will lift you up" (James 4:10, NIV). Then the apostle Peter reminds us, "Humble yourselves, therefore, under God's mighty hand, that he may lift you up in due time" (1 Pet. 5:6, NIV). There is a common theme in each of these verses: humble yourself, and God's hand will lift you up.

What happens when God lifts you up? You get a better and clearer perspective. You don't see things merely from a fleshly perspective but rather from God's point of view. This is what happened to Daniel during Israel's time under Babylonian captivity. No one could see the hand of God or what God would do. Yet Daniel fasted and prayed until God sent him a message through an angel and showed him things to come. Daniel did not live in hopelessness like the others in captivity because he fasted and got a new point of view. Daniel's fast moved the hand of God and things began to happen.

I am going to make a simple statement here: if Jesus fasted and He is the One we are following as disciples, then maybe we should take notice. Before Jesus started His public ministry, He went on a forty-day fast. What was Jesus doing? He was walking with the Lord, doing it in secret. It was during this time that Jesus had a personal encounter with Satan, who tempted Him three times. But each time, Jesus came out of the temptation in victory. To me, this illustration indicates that fasting is crucial to defeating the enemy.

Jesus's victory paints another picture of the power of fasting. When you learn to do it in secret, God will use that time in private to teach you how to defeat the enemy. It's better to learn how to fight in private than to fall in public. Fasting was the key ingredient that prepared Jesus for His encounter with Satan, and it ultimately brought about a great victory.

I want to draw your attention to another important point. When Jesus went into the fast He was already "full of the Holy Spirit." But after His fast, the Bible says, "Jesus returned to Galilee in the power of the Spirit" (Luke 4:14, NIV). There is a difference between being full of something and being immersed in something. When the Holy Spirit came upon Jesus following His baptism at the Jordan River, Jesus was then full of the Holy Spirit. But after His fast, He was "in" the power of the Spirit. Fasting is the key ingredient to moving from fullness to immersion.

This is a critical concept to grasp, so to better illustrate this, let's consider this idea through the example of a cup. You can walk over to the sink and fill a cup up to the brim. When the cup is full, the water is only on the inside of the cup. However, if you filled up the sink and dropped the cup in, not only would the cup be filled with water but it would also be totally immersed in water, inside and out. That's why Jesus told His disciples that when the Holy Spirit comes, "He dwells with you and will be in you" (John 14:17). In other words, you will be immersed; His Spirit will cover the inside and the outside. Jesus shows us the way to immersion through the act of secret fasting.

Jesus showed us the power of secret fasting and taught His disciples in the Sermon on the Mount to fast in secret (Matt. 6:16–18). We also see this practice in the Book of Acts, where we read of how God called Barnabas and Saul into the ministry (Acts 13:1–4).

WHEN SECRET FASTING REVEALS DESTINY

I wanted to wait until this chapter to share with you a very personal encounter I had with the Lord. When God called me to preach at the age of eighteen, I remember going to the altar and lying facedown. As I began to surrender to the call of God on my life, I saw a vision. In this vision the Lord showed me different phases of life and ministry that I would be part of. This vision was so real and vivid, and it's just as alive in me today as it was then.

I will not share all the details of the vision because some of it is for an appointed time yet to come. But in the vision God clearly showed me one hundred acres of property. I saw a large building and a camp. Then the Lord said in the vision, "You will pastor a movement on a hundred acres of land with a gathering place for young people and a youth camp." This is the part of the vision that gave me a strong sense of calling because it was so precise.

For three years I would draw out that property and youth camp. I would talk about it with my friends and dream big. I had no clue how it would happen, especially since at the time I was part of an inner-city ministry that had little finances and no ability to purchase that kind of property. But I kept dreaming and praying. It was at the end of those three years that God supernaturally connected me with Dr. T. L. Lowery. But even after moving to Cleveland, Tennessee, I didn't see how this vision could be fulfilled.

One year into working with Dr. Lowery, God placed on my heart the desire to start gathering with young men and women for what we called a "solemn assembly." This was just a night of praise, worship, and prayer. The most we would ever see on these nights was twenty to thirty people. The gathering was nothing big, and quite honestly, I don't think anyone expected it to grow any larger. But we were a consecrated group of people who believed God for revival in our generation and that the word of the Lord would be fulfilled in our city.

After some time we formed a small leadership group and decided to move from just worship and prayer into actual ministry of the Word. We wanted to prepare for the coming revival. It was during this time that I began to share again with some of my closer friends about the property God showed me with the gathering place for young people and the youth camp. It still seemed as crazy then as it did when I was in West Virginia. But things were about to change.

After I spent two years gathering, praying, fasting, and preaching, the Lord told me to go on a twenty-one-day fast. The Lord began stirring me in the first few days of the fast to begin to believe that God would send us a father to cover our ministry of young people. God gave me the scripture, "Behold, I will send you Elijah the prophet before the coming of the great and dreadful day of the LORD. And he will turn the hearts of the fathers to the children, and the hearts of the children to their fathers" (Mal. 4:5–6).

For ten days I prayed those scriptures, and then the Lord said, "Pray for Perry Stone's heart to be turned toward this generation." It just came from out of nowhere. I didn't really know Perry Stone. I had seen him a few times in town and knew that he served on Dr. Lowery's board of directors. I also knew that he was the Bible prophecy guy, and I figured there was no way he would be interested in fathering a bunch of crazy young people.

All of this was happening in the secrecy of my heart. As I prayed about this I decided to tell three of my closest friends what the Lord had put in my heart so that when it happened I could have someone to confirm that God had spoken this into my spirit. When I told my friends, I don't know if they even believed what God told me. But I had heard His voice in the secret place like all the other times. Once you have heard His voice, you will recognize it the rest of your life. Sometimes it seems that the weight of His voice could crush your entire body.

I prayed all the way through the fast. When the twenty-one days were over, I gradually began to eat again and continued with my weekly routine of work, service, and traveling with Dr. Lowery on the weekends. Two weeks went by, and it was time for our Tuesday night youth service. Our normal routine was for the leadership team to meet for prayer one hour before the service. As we began to pray that particular Tuesday, the glory of God filled the room. It was one of those moments when you are afraid to open your eyes because you might see God and die. It truly was a glorious moment. When we felt the release in prayer, I opened my eyes, and on the couch in our prayer room sat Perry Stone.

I walked over to greet him, and he introduced himself and said, "Mark, I need to talk with you before you go out into your service." So I sent the team out to begin worship so we could talk. We sat there, and Perry told me that God had spoken to him about thirty days earlier, which would have been the time God laid on my heart that he was supposed to father our ministry. I nearly passed out at the timing and the language that he was using, because I knew it was God.

I ran out of the room and grabbed three of my leaders and told them to tell Perry what I had told them two weeks earlier. They shared with Perry that God led me during my fast to pray for his heart to turn toward our generation. Perry was blown away by this divine confirmation, and he said to me, "When God spoke this to me I said to God that I'm just a prophecy preacher. Young people will not want anything to do with me." He said that's when God told him to go see the young man who meets with young people at the T. L. Lowery Global Ministry Center because that young man would help him lead the movement.

As if that weren't enough, God was about to really shake things up. Perry said to me, "Mark, the only thing I feel at this point that God wants to do is provide about one hundred acres so we can build a gathering place for young people and build a youth camp. And you are going to pastor this movement." At this point I was crying, and I told one of the leaders to go get my wife.

When my wife, Destani, came into the room, I shared with her what had just happened and said, "Tell Perry what I have been telling you since we got married, what the Lord said we would be a part of." She began to tell him how I would draw out the hundred-acre camp and talk about what it looked like. That's when Perry fell back on the couch. It was a moment when time and purpose collided, revealing both of our God-ordained destinies.

One of the last things Perry asked me was, "Do you need to pray about this?" I thought to myself, "No, I saw this six years ago when God called me to preach. Now the appointed time for this vision has come. I'm ready to pastor a movement." This time of fasting caused time and purpose to collide. You could say that fasting accelerated the process. That is why I titled this chapter "Fast-Forward," because practicing this secret discipline puts you on an accelerated path to your destiny.

Just like Saul and Barnabas in Acts 13:1–4, Perry and I were connected through a time of fasting. Today I'm the pastor of a movement called Omega Center International, located on one hundred acres, with a debt-free gathering place for young people that seats five thousand, and as I write this book the plans are coming together for the youth camp. If God could call me to a fast to bring all of that together, what will God do for you when you make the commitment to "do it in secret"?

I want to encourage you to not overlook the call to fast in secret. This hidden weapon not only defeats the power of the enemy in your life, protects you from those who would do you harm, and brings about divine connections with the people who will help you fulfill your God-ordained destiny, but it also has the power to change nations. Answer the call and "do it in secret" so that you're positioned to rule as a king in God's kingdom.

YOUR PARTICIPATION IS REQUIRED

W here are you? Itching for adventure? Or going nowhere very slowly? Though it may be hard to comprehend, the broad strokes of your future were sketched out long before you were born. In fact, your specific name was "called" before the universe was spoken into existence. Yet although you were on God's mind before the beginning, your life will never truly start until you choose to be chosen.

You may not be in the right place to see it just now (for "obscurity" is always God's launching pad), but all that is required to bring your future into focus is your participation and time—specifically, time alone with God. That secret place of the heart is where your most valuable relationship, your most reliable partnership, is formed. *There* is where you ask your questions. *There* is where you get your answers. *There*, in secret communion with the Creator, is where you'll find your next step on the path designed before time itself was imagined.

You may be thinking, "That may be true for most people, but I'm different." If that's how you feel, then you are "most people." We have all felt like the exception, like we don't fit in. Every individual with the ability to think has known the isolation and seclusion of being excluded. Adam and Eve were banished from Eden; David and Joseph were exiled from their families; John the Baptist was an outcast from society; even Jesus was rejected by His own people. They were all square pegs pushed aside, disregarded, and without perceived potential.

I can relate. Just a few years ago I was a no-name kid from the sticks with few skills, no experience, and no foreseeable escape from my obscure *Groundhog Day* life. Not that anyone noticed, but I was an outsider, a "misfit" going nowhere. Then someone called my name. I answered that call, made the choice to be chosen, and started off on an adventure that is still unfolding.

If God gives you a vision, He will always include the provision—the experienced pro to prepare you. In my case, God provided me with three. These spiritual mentors showed me by example how to turn irrelevance into royalty, how to transform rejection into a coronation. And it was as simple as opening my eyes to the possibilities that God has planned for us all.

Yet along that path we must be aware of the traps, for the deceiver's brand of misdirection has been time tested. His well-practiced ploy to dangle the shiniest apple over the deepest pit not only lured a third of his angelic brothers to rebel their way straight into hell, but it also tricked the first man into tasting the forbidden fruit and caused humanity to teeter on the edge of oblivion.

From the Garden of Eden to the Garden of Gethsemane, Satan has tried to misdirect mankind from heaven's plans for us. He attempted to separate us with his trick under the tree. But the Almighty's desire to fellowship with mankind could not be thwarted. First, using the temporary blood covering of animals to stay near His creation, He planned for a day when the perfect sacrifice for sins would be offered up. The essence of life that stained a wooden cross the day Jesus was crucified became the key to open the garden gate separating the Creator and His creation from their once-enjoyed walks.

And here's the kicker—the blood for that final sacrifice came from someone who had been banished—an outcast from the establishment, a person shunned by His own tribe. The blood shed on that day cascaded like a waterfall through the outcast's hair. And like the oil Samuel spilled over David's head, this flood formed a kind of crown, anointing this rejected misfit the Lord of lords and King of every tribe.

At the moment no one may know your name or how amazing you are with your slingshot, but by no means are you forgotten. The Creator knew you before your birth. In fact, God made sure you, like David, were born. He placed you on this earthly chessboard in just the right position to take advantage of your unique gifts. Your brand of greatness was tailored for the here and now. All that is required is your participation...and quality time spent in your secret place with God.

So today you have reason to rejoice, for in the fullness of time, when your moment comes to shine, the oil of heaven's favor will certainly flow. In the glow of God's light His blessing will cascade over you like a waterfall of shimmering gold. And there will be no doubt that it forms a kind of crown on your head.

When you choose to be chosen, you won't feel like a misfit much longer, because nothing fits like the crown made for you.

Don't be a square peg in this round world. Find your path, your purpose, your place. When you do, *that's* when the adventure will really begin.

NOTES

CHAPTER 1
YOU ARE CHOSEN, IF YOU CHOOSE

1. Drawn from the Midrashim; see also Chana Weisberg, "Nitzevet, the Mother of David," Chabad.org, http://www .chabad.org/theJewishWoman/article_cdo/aid/280331/jewish/ Nitzevet-Mother-of-David.htm (accessed January 23, 2015).

CHAPTER 3
PASSWORD: PASSOVER

1. Myles Munroe, *Rediscovering the Kingdom* (Shippensburg, PA: Destiny Image, 2004), xvii.

CHAPTER 5
SECRET PRAYER, PUBLIC SHADOWS

1. Andrew Murray, *With Christ in the School of Prayer* (New York: Fleming H. Revell Company, 1885), 170.

CHAPTER 6
MAKING A PRIVATE APPOINTMENT FOR PUBLIC INFLUENCE

1. For more information, see www.endtimeheadlines.org.
2. Edward M. Bounds, *Power Through Prayer* (Chicago, IL: Moody Publishers, 2009), 40.
3. As quoted in Lloyd Hildebrand, *Prayers That Change Things in Your Circumstances* (Alachua, FL: Bridge-Logos, 2013).

4. *On the Record With Greta Van Susteren*, "Rev. Billy Graham 'On the Record,' Pt. 2," Fox News video, December 20, 2010, http://video.foxnews.com/v/4469470/rev-billy-graham-on -the-record-pt-2/#sp=show-clips (accessed January 23, 2015).

5. As quoted in Eddie and Alice Smith, *Spiritual Advocates* (Lake Mary, FL: Charisma House, 2008).

CHAPTER 10
A CONVERGENCE OF GENERATIONS

1. Terry Nance, *God's Armor Bearer Volumes 1 and 2* (Springdale, AR: Focus on the Harvest, 1990).

CHAPTER 11
GIVING IS WORTH MORE IN SECRET

1. Randy Alcorn, *The Treasure Principle* (Colorado Springs, CO: Multnomah Books, 2001), 51.

CONTACT

mark **casto**

P.O. Box 3411
Cleveland, TN 37320
www.markcasto.com